EARLY YEARS
AROUND THE YEAR

Personal, social and emotional development
Seasonal activities

Jean Evans

Seasonal ideas • Festival activities • Early learning goals

CREDITS

British Library Cataloguing-in-Publication Data
A catalogue record for this book is available from the British Library.

ISBN 0 439 01911 7

Every effort has been made to trace copyright holders and the publishers apologize for any inadvertent omissions.

AUTHOR
Jean Evans

EDITOR
Clare Miller

ASSISTANT EDITOR
Saveria Mezzana

SERIES DESIGNER
Anna Oliwa

DESIGNER
Paul Roberts

ILLUSTRATIONS
Anna Hopkins

COVER ILLUSTRATION
Anna Hopkins

ACKNOWLEDGEMENTS
The publishers gratefully acknowledge permission to reproduce the following copyright material:

Sally Scott for the use of 'Dragon drama' and 'Winter song' by Sally Scott, music arranged from traditional songs © 2001, Sally Scott, both previously unpublished.

Qualifications and Curriculum Authority for the use of extracts from the QCA/DfEE document *Curriculum Guidance for the foundation stage* © 2000, Qualifications and Curriculum Authority.

Text © 2001 Jean Evans
© 2001 Scholastic Ltd

Published by Scholastic Ltd, Villiers House, Clarendon Avenue, Leamington Spa, Warwickshire CV32 5PR

Designed using Adobe Pagemaker
Printed by Proost NV, Belgium

Visit our website at www.scholastic.co.uk

1 2 3 4 5 6 7 8 9 0   1 2 3 4 5 6 7 8 9 0

INTRODUCTION

BACKGROUND INFORMATION

SPRING

SUMMER

Around the year

The aims of the series

The *Around the Year* series provides practical activities to support children's progress through the Stepping Stones towards the Early Learning Goals for each of the six areas of learning. The books provide a collection of ideas to use throughout the year based on both seasonal opportunities and dates linked to a range of multicultural festivals. Each book provides a wealth of activity ideas supported by photocopiable resources, including activity sheets, templates, poems, songs and stories. Although the activities are aimed at four-year-olds, the 'Support' section gives suggestions about how the main activity can be adapted for younger children or those with special needs, and the 'Extension' section explains how the main activity can be extended for older or more able children. The ideas suggested can be applied equally well to the documents on pre-school education published for Scotland, Wales and Northern Ireland.

Personal, social and emotional development

This book focuses on children's personal, social and emotional development, an area of learning often implicit within an early years setting rather than specifically planned for. One of the aims of the book is to emphasize the need to plan specifically for this learning area and also to consider the Early Learning Goals for Personal, social and emotional development during activities related to other learning areas and daily routines, such as 'snack time'. The book gives examples of how this can be achieved through regular festivals and events throughout the year.

How to use this book

The activities are organized into four chapters, one for each season, and

every chapter is subdivided into eight festival-based and six seasonal-based activities. The Early Learning Goals have been used as the learning objectives for activities and a good balance has been achieved across the goals for the whole learning area. Practitioners can be assured that, if they follow the suggested activities, they will provide opportunities for the children to work successfully towards these goals. As personal, social and emotional development underpins all of the planning and organization of an early years setting, many of the activities would seem to be related to another area, for example, a science-based activity observing life cycles or a mathematical activity involving sorting and matching objects. However, in all the activities in this book, whatever their apparent subject bias, a clear learning objective from the early learning goals for personal social and emotional development has been identified.

The activities in this book are categorized in the same way as those of the rest of the series to assist staff with forward planning and provide continuity if several books are being used at once.

As the Early Learning Goals are designed to cover the Foundation Stage from three to five years, there needs to be some element of differentiation included in the activities. The book aims to achieve this with the 'Support' and 'Extension' paragraphs, which include Stepping Stones across each goal. Following these suggestions will help children to work towards these goals in manageable stages at their own pace.

Where an activity involves cooking or handling of food, this symbol will remind you to check for any allergies and dietary requirements.

Seasons and festivals

The aim of the seasonal activities is to start with the children's direct experiences of their world and the familiar changes in weather and living things. The activities are intended to be flexible. They can form part of a larger theme on a particular season or simply be chosen in isolation, perhaps stimulated by a child's observation or a favourite story.

Details of each festival are given in brief at the start of the book with the aim of assisting forward planning and extending background knowledge. The main religious festivals are included as well as several special days and secular events. Some festivals are common to all books in the series to provide continuity and the opportunity to plan a theme across all six areas of learning.

Photocopiable pages

The aim of the photocopiable pages is to assist staff rather than to provide the children with 'time fillers'. They are not intended to be used by the children on their own. The outlines for matching cards present staff with a variety of options for creating games linked to the activities. The outlines for the children to cut and stick are intended to be used as an adult-led group activity to develop social skills. The rhyme sheets introduce new rhymes, directly related to the activities, and can be used by staff and also copied to send home to share with parents and carers. The song sheets are also original and based on a favourite tune to stimulate the practitioners and the children to try making up songs of their own. They, too, can be copied and sent home. Observation sheets are intended to be informative, stimulate discussion and develop concentration skills. A gameboard is included to support one of the activities and also to encourage the practitioners to try further ideas for simple games.

Home links are suggested so that the activities can be developed at home to encourage parents and carers and staff to share and continue to create appropriate learning opportunities for the children.

Festivals

St David's Day (1 March)
The feast day of St David, the patron saint of Wales. The people of Wales enjoy a cultural festival of national song and music and wear a daffodil or leek.

Mother's Day (March/April)
This special day is a time when mothers, and others who have similar caring roles, are thanked with presents and cards.

Holi (March/April)
A Hindu festival that takes place as a reminder of how God protects His believers. Hindus throw paint and coloured water over one another and dance through the streets to remember the mischief of the young Krishna.

Easter (March/April)
An important festival in the Christian calendar marking the time when Jesus rose from the dead. Eggs are associated with Easter because they symbolize new life and beginnings.

Pesach/Passover (March/April)
This is a Jewish festival that celebrates the time when Moses led the Israelites from slavery in Egypt to Israel, the Promised Land. A traditional meal called Seder is eaten.

Baisakhi (14 April)
This is an important Sikh celebration that commemorates the time when five volunteers sacrificed themselves at the request of Guru Gobind Singh. They became the first select group or Khalsa.

Hanamatsuri (April)
A Japanese flower festival that celebrates the birth of Buddha. Images of the baby Buddha are placed on small stands and decorated with flowers, to symbolize the garden in which the Buddha was born.

May Day (1 May)
In the past, May Day celebrated the start of summer. Traditionally, a maypole would be erected on a village green and a 'Queen of May' would be chosen.

Wesak (May/June)
This festival marks the birth, death and enlightenment of the Buddha. People decorate their homes and temples with flowers, candles, lanterns and incense.

Midsummer's Day (24 June)
Falls shortly after the longest day of the year. It is a time when fairies and witches are said to come out. Traditions include bonfires, feasts and torchlit processions.

Father's Day (June)
A special day to acknowledge the role of fathers and others who have similar caring roles. They are thanked with presents and cards.

Pentecost (June)
In the Christian calendar, it celebrates the day when the Holy Spirit came to Jesus' disciples and inspired them to continue the work of Jesus.

Dragon Boat Festival (June)
This festival is a reminder of when the popular Chinese leader, Ch'u Yuan, drowned himself. Followers raced down the river in dragon boats making loud noises and throwing rice to stop the fish from eating him.

St Swithun's Day (15 July)
It is said that if it rains on St Swithun's Day it will rain for a further 40 days.

Janamashtami (July/August/September)
This is a Hindu festival that celebrates the birth of Lord Krishna. Hindus fast

during the day and enjoy celebrations at midnight to welcome the baby Krishna. A statue or picture of Krishna is placed in a cradle and everyone files past to rock the cradle.

Ganesh-chaturthi (August/September)
This festival commemorates the birthday of Ganesh, the elephant-headed god of wisdom and prosperity. It is celebrated on the fourth day of the Hindu month, Bhadrapada.

Grandparent's Day (September)
This is a modern festival in which children and families acknowledge the role of grandparents and thank them by making cards and sending them presents.

Rosh Hashana (September/October)
This is the Jewish New Year. It begins ten days of repentance and self-examination with the blowing of the ram's horn, or 'shofar', to remember how Abraham sacrificed a ram instead of his son, Isaac.

Harvest Festival (September/October)
It is a time of thanksgiving for the harvesting of crops. Traditions include harvest suppers and giving of food to the needy.

Yom Kippur (September/October)
The Day of Atonement, nine days after Rosh Hashana. It is the holiest day in the Jewish year, with 24 hours of fasting, praying and asking for forgiveness for sins. A 'shofar' is blown at the end of the festival.

Divali (October/November)
This is the Hindu New Year festival. It is a festival of lights to honour Lakshmi, goddess of wealth and prosperity.

St Andrew's Day (30 November)
The feast day for the patron saint of Scotland. A traditional meal of haggis, neeps and tatties is eaten.

Guru Nanak's birthday (November)
Sikh festival celebrating the birthday of Guru Nanak, the founder of the faith. A meal is shared from the free kitchen and distributed to the poor and needy.

Hanukkah (November/December)
The eight-day Jewish festival of light held to commemorate the story of how the Jews overcame the Syrians and returned to their desecrated temple.

Ramadan (November/December)
This festival is held on the ninth month of the Muslim year and is one of the Five Pillars of Islam. The days of this month are marked by fasting between dawn and sunset.

Christmas Day (25 December)
The Christian festival celebrating the birth of Jesus.

Eid-ul-Fitr (December/January)
Muslim festival marking the end of the month of fasting, Ramadan, and a time of special prayers, family celebrations and the exchange of gifts.

New Year (1 January)
Celebrated in the western world with parties on the last night of December. People reflect on the past and make resolutions for the future.

Ganjitsu (1 January)
The Japanese New Year. The festival is both solemn and joyful. Money is given to the children, new clothes are worn and family games are played.

St Valentine's Day (14 February)
People celebrate this day by sending cards and gifts to their loved ones.

Shrove Tuesday (February/March)
The day before the Christian season of Lent begins. Cupboards are cleared and pancakes are traditionally made to use up some of the foods to be given up during the fasting period of Lent.

Signs of spring

What you need
Outdoor clothing, such as coats, hats, gloves, scarves and boots; frieze paper; set of indoor clothing; card; staple gun (adult use).

What to do
Talk to the children about signs of spring after the cold dark season of winter. Explain to them how buds start opening to reveal new leaves and how many baby animals are born at this time of year. Create a display by drawing around a child, cutting around the outline and attaching it to a display board in the cloakroom area. Dress the outline in indoor clothes attached with staples. Attach items of outdoor clothing around it. Label all the items clearly.

Suggest that the children go outdoors and, if possible, walk to a local park or woodland to look for signs of spring. Look out of the window and discuss the weather. Ask the children what they think they should wear to go outside. Refer to the display when the children are preparing for outdoors, pointing to each item in turn. Discuss with the group which items of outdoor clothing on the display would be the most appropriate for the weather that day. Encourage the children to put on appropriate clothing by themselves.

Once outside, observe signs of new life, such as buds on plants and flowers or green leaves on trees. After returning to the nursery, encourage the children to talk about how they felt in their outdoor clothing. Ask them if they were too hot, too cold or just right. What do they think they could wear to make

them warmer/cooler? Refer to the wall display again and invite the children to point to the appropriate items as they answer your question.

Support
Teach the children the names of all the items on the display and point out the different forms of fasteners, such as zips, buttons and laces. Encourage older children to help younger children to put on their outdoor clothes and fasten them up.

Extension
Invite the children to collect fallen items such as leaves, sticks and twigs to make spring collage pictures. Cut out pictures of children in appropriate clothing from catalogues and stick them onto the pictures.

Learning objective
To dress and undress independently.

Group size
Depends on the number of adults available to supervise the children: ideally, one adult to two children.

Home links
Ask parents and carers to bring in their children's outdoor clothing for the trip outdoors. Invite volunteers to help with supervision on the walk.

Budding artists

Learning objective
To maintain attention, concentrate and sit quietly when appropriate.

Group size
Up to six children.

What you need

Coloured paint; paintbrushes; coloured paper; crayons; scrap collage materials; glue; scissors; green frieze paper; budding branches; three tables; books about spring with pictures of buds.

What to do

Look at books about spring together and talk about the changes that happen in nature. Go outside your setting with the children and look for signs of spring. Point out buds and newly opening leaves to the children. Encourage them to handle twigs, buds and leaves and look closely at them through magnifying glasses. How are they different? Tell the children the names of different tree parts.

Back at your setting, set up three tables, one with paint, one with crayons and another with collage materials and glue. Ensure that each table has an ample supply of paper in a range of colours. Place the budding branches and the books about spring in the middle of each table. Explain to the children that they can decide whether they would prefer to paint, draw or create a collage picture of a bud. Encourage them to sit quietly, concentrate and look closely at one of the buds from the middle of the table before starting their picture.

Once the pictures are finished, cut each child's picture into the shape of a leaf and stick it onto some green frieze paper to make a display of the children's work. Older children can add their own names.

Support

Praise the children positively for their attempts and do not worry about accuracy. It is more important that they feel confident and satisfied as they make their first observational drawings than that they create recognizable pictures. Write their names on the pictures for them.

Extension

Talk about evergreen trees, explaining that not all trees lose their leaves in autumn. Ask the children if they know the names of any evergreen trees. When walking outdoors, look out for examples of evergreen trees, such as holly.

Home links
Ask parents and carers to bring in small branches from trees in their gardens. Compare the different samples at nursery and use them to create a display table about trees.

Caring for seeds

What you need
Small plant pots or yoghurt pots; large tray; teaspoons; mixed seeds to plant; watering can; large sheet of paper; pen; compost; lollipop sticks; several copies of the photocopiable sheet on page 65.

Preparation
Copy the photocopiable sheet several times onto card and colour the pictures. Laminate each sheet and cut into four.

What to do
Talk to the children about planting seeds, and explain that these need regular attention, such as watering, to help them grow. Explain that all living things need water and air in order to grow. Play games using the cards you have made from the photocopiable sheet to reinforce the children's understanding of how seeds grow into plants and to develop their group skills.

Give sets of cards to individual children and ask them to arrange the pictures in the correct sequence. Use several sets of the cards to play games turning them over to collect matching pairs and sets of four showing each stage.

Provide each child with a plant pot or yoghurt pot. Place a large tray of compost in the centre of the table and invite the children to use teaspoons to fill their pots. Ask them to poke a hole into the soil, choose a seed to put into it and cover it over. Place a named lollipop stick in each pot so that the children can identify their seeds as these grow.

Place the pots on a window sill or other bright sheltered surface. Explain to the children that their seeds will need light from the sun in order to grow, as well as water. Make a chart labelled with the days of the week from Monday to Friday. Divide the children's names between the days on the chart. Check the name each day and ask the corresponding child to water all the plants and make sure that they are healthy.

Try planting seeds in various different textures, such as a pot of pebbles, sand, sawdust or dried pasta. Follow the same watering routine as used for the seeds potted in compost. Record the growth of the plants, if any, and talk about why some may have grown when others have not.

Support
Help the children to write their names on the labels. Offer supervision in the watering of the plants and point out what to look for when checking the health of the plants.

Extension
Encourage the children to name their own lollipop sticks, record the growth of the plants every week by measuring or drawing a weekly picture, and record the results in a chart.

Learning objective
To work as part of a group, sharing and taking turns.

Group size
Five children.

Home links
Invite donations of seeds, small pots for planting them and empty seed packets for discussion time. Invite a keen gardener to come and talk about how seeds are planted and cared for.

Find the baby

What you need
Pictures of adult animals; small plastic models of corresponding animal babies; glue; card; scissors; large draw-string bag; several copies of the photocopiable sheet on page 66.

Preparation
Copy the photocopiable sheet several times onto pieces of card. Colour the pictures and cut them into individual cards. Find appropriate pictures of adult animals in magazines, cut these out and stick them onto card. Laminate all the cards for protection.

What to do
Talk to the children about the appearance of new life in spring, such as leaves on the trees, birds building nests and lambs in the fields. Sit together in a circle, with the pictures of the adult animals face upwards in the centre. Fill the draw-string bag with the model animals. Choose a child to feel in the bag and pull out an animal.

Ask them to name the baby animal and to point out its different features to the rest of the group before putting the model on top of the appropriate picture of the adult animal. Pass the bag to the next child and continue until all the pictures have a matching baby and each child has had a turn to speak in front of the rest of the group. Alternatively, use the cards from the photocopiable sheet to play the game, putting the baby animal cards in the bag and the adult animal cards in the centre of the circle.

Try to think of rhymes about the different animals, such as 'Baa Baa Black Sheep' or 'This Little Pig', and say them together before inviting volunteers to stand up and say the rhyme on their own. Encourage the children to take turns to choose a favourite animal and tell the rest of the group the reasons for the choice made.

The photocopiable sheet could also be used to play additional matching and sorting games.

Learning objective
To be confident to try new activities, initiate ideas and speak in front of a group.

Group size
Up to six children.

Home links
Send home a copy of the photocopiable sheet for the children to cut out with their parents or carers to play a matching game at home. Ask parents and carers to take their children into the country to look for signs of new life, such as lambs and bird's nests.

Support
Help the children to become familiar with the names of the animals and their babies.

Extension
Enjoy playing 'I spy' with the models, the pictures or the cards from the photocopiable sheet. Put some appropriate letter cards in the 'feely bag', and make up the picture cards using the photocopiable sheet. Encourage the children to try to find an animal or baby animal starting with the letter pulled out of the bag.

An indoor walk

This is an ideal activity for those who do not have access to outdoors, but will be equally useful for any group when poor weather prevents outings.

What you need
Large sheet of paper; fabric; indoor apparatus; chairs.

What to do
Ensure that as large a space as possible is cleared and use furniture and equipment to improvise a scene. For example, create a pond from blue fabric, trees from chairs and a path from carpet tiles.

Talk to the children about the signs of spring and make a list (either writing or drawing) on a large piece of paper of things that they might see on a walk. Suggest that they go on a pretend walk together to look for

the things they have listed. Explain that they will have to cross a busy road and that they should have a friend to hold hands with. Invite them to pretend to put on outdoor clothing, then let them get into their pairs and walk around the room to find a suitable place to 'cross the road'.

Continue to the clear space and encourage the children to use their imagination by making your own suggestions first. For example, pretend to see a bird building a nest and ask the children to be the birds flying around the room in search of food.

Encourage them to work in pairs to build a nest together. Suggest that they become tadpoles swimming in a pond, buds opening on trees, rabbits hopping and lambs jumping in the fields. Refer to the list made at the start of the activity and include any of the children's ideas. Sing favourite songs and rhymes at appropriate points, such as 'Baa Baa Black Sheep' and 'Five Little Speckled Frogs'. Finally, get back into pairs and walk back across the 'road' to the nursery.

Support
Focus on just one aspect of spring at a time and make the activity simpler – for example, pretend to be lambs in the fields.

Extension
Make a miniature version of your walk for small-world people in a shallow tray, using model animals and natural materials such as soil, pebbles and twigs.

Learning objective
To work as part of a group and to form good relationships.

Home links
Send home a sheet of your chosen springtime songs and rhymes for families to share at home. Invite parents to listen to the children's springtime songs and rhymes.

Miniature gardens

Learning objective
To show care and concern for living things and for the environment.

Group size
Up to six children.

What you need
Compost; moss; soil; grass seeds; small plastic ice-cream container; trowels; model frogs; bubble wrap; black plastic sack; small-world people; baby bath or water tray; small pebbles; flat stones; twigs; pink and white tissues; glue; waterproof black felt-tipped pen.

What to do
Talk to the children about the different forms of new life that they might see in their gardens or on walks in the springtime. Suggest that they might like to make a miniature garden so that the small-world people can enjoy their own springtime. Discuss what will be in the garden.

Fill a baby bath or water tray with a layer of small pebbles and then cover this with a mixture of compost and soil. Form a hole in the centre and drop the ice-cream container into this. Add some pebbles to the bottom of the container and fill it almost to the top with water to create a pond. Make paths out of flat stones. Glue some screwed-up tissue to the twigs to represent blossom and push the twigs firmly into the soil to make trees. Make frog spawn from bubble wrap by drawing a black spot in the centre of each bubble and float it on the pond. Cut out some plastic tadpoles from the black refuse sack and let them swim in the pond. Arrange the frogs around the edge of the pond on pebbles. Sprinkle

some grass seeds on the soil and water daily. Add other seeds, carrot tops and model creatures to develop your springtime theme.

Once the grass has started to grow, cut it regularly with scissors. Talk to the children about the importance of caring for growing things and protecting wildlife in general.

When the garden is established, let the children play freely and make up stories with the small-world people.

Support
Give the children small, easily managed tools with which to help you fill the container with soil and compost. Support the children as necessary with the activities, such as making frog spawn and blossom

Extension
Let the children create individual gardens in small seed trays.

Home links
Ask parents and carers to take their children out to look for signs of spring. Invite them to donate items and seeds for the miniature garden.

Making music

Learning objective
To be confident to try new activities and speak in a familiar group.

Group size
Whole group for discussion and Eisteddfod festival; six children at a time to make instruments.

What you need
Empty plastic bottles; dried pulses; pasta or small stones; large buttons or beads; string; elastic bands; empty ice-cream containers; sticky tape.

What to do
Explain that St David is the Patron Saint of Wales and that on St David's Day, Welsh Christians celebrate their nationality with an Eisteddfod – a festival of music and song. Ask the children if they have ever been to a concert or seen somebody singing or playing an instrument. Suggest to the children that they make their own musical instruments for an Eisteddfod at their own setting.

Arrange small containers of the various items on a table and ask each child to choose an empty plastic bottle and something from one of the containers to put into it. Talk about quantities and encourage the children to experiment with how much to put in the bottle in order to create the best sound effects. When they are happy with the resulting sound they have created, put the bottle-tops back on and secure them tightly. Make 'bells' with the children by helping them to thread large buttons or beads onto small lengths of string. Attach the string to sticks so that the buttons hit each other when the sticks are shaken.

Make 'guitar' sound boxes by asking the children to stretch various elastic bands around open ice-cream containers. Secure the elastic bands to the side of the container with tape. Ask the children to pluck the bands to see if they all sound the same.

Enjoy your Welsh Eisteddfod together. Encourage each child to stand in front of the group to sing their favourite song and ask the other children to play along with their home-made instruments.

Support
Encourage shy children to sing by joining in with them or playing an instrument beside them.

Extension
Let the children decorate their home-made instruments with coloured paints and collage materials. Help them to compare the look and sound of their home-made instruments with real instruments.

Home links
Ask the children to bring in any musical instruments they may have at home. Invite parents and carers to watch the children perform their Eisteddfod and to join in by playing an instrument if they can.

Scented cards

What you need:
Selection of rectangles of coloured card in varying sizes; colourful tissue-paper discs; green sticky paper; PVA glue; glue spreaders; sheets of white paper; small containers of talcum powder; selection of perfumes; herbs; spices; felt-tipped pens.

What to do
Begin by talking about Mother's Day and asking the children about their mother, carer or a special person in their lives. Remain sensitive to individual circumstances. Suggest that the children make a card for that special person.

Invite the children to choose a piece of coloured card, fold it in half and draw, on the inside, a picture of the recipient of the card, using the felt-tipped pens. Encourage the children to make a flower picture on the front of the card using the materials on the table, for example, tissue-paper discs for flowers and green sticky paper for leaves and stalks. Emphasize that the choice of materials is their own.

Talk to the children about how they could make the tissue-paper flowers smell like real flowers. Arrange the selection of perfumes and scented items on the table. Give each child one of the dry items to sprinkle onto a clean sheet of paper. Ask them to smell the different pieces of paper and choose the scent that they like best. Emphasize that they must not put their noses too close to the paper. Invite each child to spread a thin layer of PVA glue across the tissue of their 'flower' and to sprinkle their chosen item over it. Put a dab of each of the perfumes on separate pieces of paper and ask the children to smell them and choose one. Add a drop of the chosen perfume to the centre of each flower.

Invite the children to close their eyes, smell the finished cards and talk about whether they smell like real flowers. Can they tell you what the different smells remind them of?

Support
Provide the children with fewer options and more distinctive smells.

Extension
As an alternative to cards, suggest to the children that they try to make perfumed pictures in card frames using the same technique.

EARLY YEARS AROUND THE YEAR Personal, social and emotional development

Splashing out!

Learning objective
To respond to significant experiences, showing a range of feelings.

Group size
Up to six children.

What you need
Plain paper; gingerbread-man cutters or cardboard templates of people; pencils or crayons; scissors; magazines; glue; several colours of powder paint in pots; paintbrushes; icing sugar; bowl of water.

What to do
Begin by talking to the children about how people remember the story of Lord Krishna by running through the streets throwing coloured water and paint over one another. Ask the children how it would feel to be splashed with coloured paints and water, and discuss other occasions when the children have been splashed, such as bathtime, in the rain and at the swimming-pool.

Ask the children to draw carefully around the gingerbread-man cutters or cardboard templates onto pieces of plain paper and colour them in. Alternatively, the children could cut out characters from magazines and glue them onto the paper.

Help the children to mix some icing sugar in a bowl of water until it dissolves and then cover the paper with a coating of the solution. Show them how to carefully sprinkle or scatter the different colours of dry powder paint over the paper.

Encourage the children to 'splash' their characters with various colours and to watch as the powder spreads across the wet paper. Discuss the effects. What happens when colours merge? Which colours make the best patterns? Which ones look most effective?

Make some cards using the same technique of cut-out outlines. Write a simple version of the story of Lord Krishna and make copies of it to stick inside the cards. Let the children take them home and share the story and traditions of Holi with their families.

Support
Provide the children with a cut-out character ready to stick onto the paper.

Extension
Help the children to bake gingerbread men and decorate them with splashes of multicoloured icing.

Home links
Ask the children to bring items from home that they would wear on a wet day to stop them from getting wet or splashed, such as a raincoat, umbrella, hat and boots. Take buckets and bowls of water outside and have fun wearing the clothes and imitating rain showers by splashing one another.

Fun with eggs

Learning objective
To become familiar with and share traditions associated with festivals from their own culture and to expect others to treat those traditions with respect.

Group size
Large group for discussion and egg races; groups of six for rolling activity.

What you need
Hard-boiled eggs; coloured felt-tipped pens or paint; various sizes of spoons; table tennis balls; building bricks; an enlarged copy of the photocopiable sheet on page 67.

What to do
Talk to the children about Easter traditions, including the one of rolling decorated eggs down a hill. Say the Easter rhymes 'Five Easter eggs' and 'Easter is here!' on the photocopiable sheet together. Make five egg-shaped

finger puppets and remove them one at a time to accompany the first rhyme. Sing the second rhyme to the tune of 'Frère Jacques' and encourage the children to join in to perform the actions with you.

Invite the children to decorate the hard-boiled eggs with colourful patterns using felt-tipped pens and to experiment with dyeing them, for

example, with onion skins. Varnish the eggs to protect the design.

Take the children to a gently sloping area outdoors if possible, or create one indoors, for example, by lowering the height of a slide. Ask the children to take turns to roll their eggs down the slope. Talk about the shape of the eggs and whether they will roll in a straight line. Have egg-and-spoon races with the children, either indoors or outdoors. Look at different-sized spoons with the children and ask them to try different ones to balance their eggs on. Let them select a size of spoon that the egg balances on most easily and encourage them to talk about why this might be.

Make a wide tunnel shape using building bricks and invite the children to try and roll their eggs through it. Talk to them about the shape of an egg and why it is difficult to roll it in a straight line.

Give the children table-tennis balls and encourage them to repeat the exercise. Ask them which item is easiest to roll into the tunnel. Talk about round and oval shapes. Encourage the children to think of other objects which are round or oval.

Support
Make sure that the children have spoons of a manageable size and that the tunnels are not too narrow so that they can be confident of some success.

Extension
Introduce the children to other shapes to try and roll, such as cubes and cylinders. Encourage them to put forward ideas as to why some objects will not roll.

Home links
Ask parents and carers to prepare a hard-boiled egg for their child to bring to nursery for the activity. Send home a list of suggestions for different ways of dyeing hard-boiled eggs.

A spicy treat

What you need
Two apples; half a cup of apple juice; half a cup of crushed walnuts; teaspoon of cinnamon; tablespoon of chopped dates and raisins; teaspoon; small serving bowls and spoons; cheese grater; mixing bowl; rolling pin; plastic bag.

What to do
Explain to the children that Pesach (also known as Passover) is an important Jewish festival where families come together and enjoy a traditional feast. During the meal, fathers tell their young children the story of how Moses parted the Red Sea to guide the Jews from Egypt to Israel, from slavery to freedom. A sweet called Charoset, made from fruit and nuts, is served at the Pesach meal to remind the Jews of the sweetness of freedom.

Grate two apples into the mixing bowl. Place the nuts in a plastic bag and ask the children to help crush the nuts with a rolling pin. Measure half a cup of crushed nuts with the children and add this to the bowl, along with the teaspoon of cinnamon.

Encourage the children to help you measure a tablespoon of chopped dates and raisins and put them in the bowl. Add half a cup of apple juice and invite the children to stir the mixture. Finally, help them to spoon individual servings into small bowls for everyone in the group.

Support
Children who find it difficult to be involved in the measuring exercises of the activity can help by giving the mixture a final stir.

Extension
Talk to the children about different measurements, such as the difference between a whole cup and half a cup. Encourage them to compare different spoon sizes.

Learning objectives
To begin to recognize their own needs, feelings and views and to be sensitive to those of others; to express likes and dislikes in a group.

Group size
Large group for discussion and six children for the activity.

Home links
Ask parents and carers to bring in items from home for the Charoset. Ask families from other religions to bring in traditional recipes and perhaps help to prepare them at your setting. Invite any Jewish parents to come and talk to the children about Pesach.

Fly the flag

Learning objective
To form good relationships with adults and peers and feel part of the group.

Group size
Large group for discussion, four children to make the flags.

What you need
Potatoes or sponges; old white sheet cut into rectangles (about 20cm x 10cm); sticks; garden canes; coloured paint; coloured beads; laces; sticky tape; newly opened buds.

Preparation
Invite carers to send in examples of uniforms, and make a display. Cut sponges or potatoes into 'K' shapes.

What to do
Discuss how it feels to belong to a special group and ask the children if they have any older brothers or sisters who wear a uniform. Look at pictures of flags and national emblems. Talk to the children about the Sikh tradition of the 'Five Ks': Kesh (uncut beard and hair), Kangha (comb), Kara (steel bracelet), Kirpan (short sword) and Kachera (pair of shorts).

Ask each child to decide on their favourite colour from a selection of coloured beads and encourage them to thread a bead of that colour onto a lace with the end tied to secure it.

Talk with the children about which colour was the most popular and suggest that they use the 'Five Ks' on flags for the nursery, using this colour to make the prints on the flags. Help each child to print five 'K's onto a rectangle of white fabric using one of the pre-cut potato or sponge shapes, counting aloud as they make each print. Once the fabric is dry, attach it with sticky tape to pre-cut lengths of cane.

Have fun with the flags. Take them outdoors on a windy day or have a parade with them, marching to music and waving them in the air. Decorate the nursery entrance with the flags for Baisakhi, or arrange them around a display about the festival.

Support
Let the children practise printing on paper first to develop the skill.

Extension
Play 'Stations', with the children pretending to be trains. Designate each

corner of the room with a different colour. Choose a child to hold a flag up to signal 'stop'. When the flag is held up, the children must choose a colour and move to the corresponding corner of the room. The child with the flag then calls out one of the four colours and all those in that station must sit at the side of the room. The game continues until all the children are sitting down.

Home links
Ask parents and carers to bring in items from home that start with the letter 'K' to create a 'K table'. Invite someone who wears a uniform to talk to the children about the items they wear and why.

Baby Buddha

Learning objective
To become aware of their own culture and to begin to understand that people have different views, cultures and beliefs which need to be treated with respect.

Group size
Whole group for discussion; up to six children to make the cribs.

What you need
Selection of boxes such as shoeboxes; small dolls; collage materials; scissors; pictures of plants and flowers; glue; coloured fabric; white fabric; salt dough; plastic vases and flowers; tissue paper; string; favourite doll; doll's cot.

What to do
Begin by talking about how the baby Buddha was born in a flower garden and make comparisons with how baby Jesus was born in a stable. Ask the children if they know where they were born and talk about their memories of any births in their families.

Invite each child to make a crib for the baby Buddha by decorating a small box with colourful collage materials. Ask them to choose pictures of flowers and plants to cut out and stick to the side of their crib. Place a piece of coloured material into each crib and a small doll to represent the baby Buddha. Alternatively, dolls can be especially made from cardboard tubes or salt dough. Wrap all the dolls in white sheeting.

Cover a doll's cot with garlands of tissue-paper discs threaded to string, wrap a favourite nursery doll in a white sheet and put it in the cot to represent the baby Buddha. Stand the cot at the front of a table display of the children's cribs, along with vases of flowers.

Support
Ask older children to help the younger children cut out pictures of flowers for their cribs. Use petal confetti or tissue-paper discs to create a simpler flower effect on the boxes.

Extension
Let older children make 3-D flowers to decorate their cribs with, using egg-box sections, bottle tops, coloured pipe-cleaners and tissue paper. Encourage them to line the inside of their boxes by measuring and cutting out appropriate pieces of fabric and sticking these carefully to the insides.

Home links
Ask a parent or carer with a baby to visit your setting and talk about where the baby was born. Ask families to bring in flowers from home and display them in vases among the children's home-made cribs to create an attractive flower-garden effect.

Maypole dancing

What you need
Large pole such as an extendable mop handle or broom handle; lengths of coloured ribbon; Christmas-tree holder or large bucket; stones; masking tape; a copy of the photocopiable sheet on page 68 for each child; various pieces of music.

What to do
Talk to the children about how May Day is celebrated by Christians on 1 May. Look at some pictures of village maypoles and May Day celebrations. Explain how, many years ago, villagers would select a young tall tree, stripping off its lower branches and leaving the higher ones to represent new life. They would stand this in the middle of the village green and use it as a maypole.

Give each child a photocopiable sheet and look at the picture together as you talk about maypoles. Ask them to move their fingers along each ribbon to find out whose ribbon the bird has flown off with.

Help the children to create a maypole in your setting. Support the large pole so that it stands upright. If possible, use a Christmas-tree holder or a bucket filled with large stones, to ensure that the pole is very stable. Attach long coloured ribbons to the top of the pole using masking tape. Play some music, ask each child to take a ribbon and invite the children to skip around the maypole, all in the same direction. When the ribbons are too short, ask the children to turn around and skip in the opposite direction around the maypole.

Talk to the children about dances from other cultures, such as Scottish country dancing. Play some music from another culture and ask the children to make up their own dances around the maypole. Invite alternate children to dance one way while the others dance in the opposite direction, then let everyone swap and dance the opposite way. Try different ideas, such as some children standing still while others dance under them. What happens to the ribbon pattern around the pole? Is it always the same?

Support
Invite the children to dance around the room or the maypole waving ribbons in the air rather than holding ribbons attached to the maypole.

Extension
Talk to the children about different types of dance, such as ballet and tap-dancing, and hold a 'mini concert' with each child, or small groups of children, performing their own imaginative dances.

Seaside role-play

What you need
Paddling pool; large plastic sheet; dry sand; stones; shells; green Cellophane; selection of clothes and outdoor objects, such as buckets and spades, towels, sunglasses, beach balls, swimwear, gloves, hats, wellington boots and umbrellas.

Preparation
Blow up the paddling pool and cut out some strips of green Cellophane.

What to do
Talk to the children about going on a trip to the beach and ask them to think about the sort of items they would take with them and the clothing that they would wear.

Create a 'seaside' in the nursery by putting a paddling pool in a large space with the plastic sheet on the ground in front of it. Pour dry sand over the plastic sheet and ask the children to arrange shells and stones on the sand. Let them fill the paddling pool and put the green Cellophane into the water to create a seaweed effect. Place your selection of various outdoor objects on the floor beside the seaside scene.

Spread beach towels in front of the sand and role-play being on a trip to the beach. Help the children to change into beachwear and ask each child to select something from the items on the floor that they feel would be suitable to take on a day at the beach. Sit on the towels and ask the children to take turns to explain the reasons for their

choices. Look at the items left behind and ask the children why they think these things are unsuitable to take to the beach.

Support
Encourage older children to offer suggestions when younger children are choosing an item to take to the beach. Offer plenty of assistance to the children in putting on their beachwear.

Extension
Make a simple counting exercise for the children by selecting stones and shells from the sandy area in front of the paddling pool. Invite each child to take a turn at throwing a stone into the water, counting each stone together as it is thrown. Repeat the exercise with the shells. Did they count the same number of shells and pebbles?

Pack a suitcase

Learning objective
To maintain attention, concentrate and sit quietly when appropriate.

Group size
Groups of six children.

What you need
Items suitable for taking on a summer holiday, such as bucket and spade, sun-hat, beachwear, towels and sun-glasses; items which are not usually taken on a summer holiday, such as a woolly hat, scarf, gloves and thick coat; large suitcase; a copy of the photocopiable sheet on page 69 for each child; child-safe scissors.

Preparation
Gather together all of the items and put them in the suitcase.

What to do
Put the suitcase in the middle of the group and ask the children to

sit in a circle around it. Explain that the case is very heavy and talk about what might be inside it. What are cases used for? Talk about times that the children have used cases. Open the case and empty all of the contents out onto the floor around it.

Tell the children that you are planning to go on holiday to the seaside and that you want them to help you pack the things you will need. Take turns to choose something suitable and talk about the reason for your choice before putting it back into the suitcase.

Emphasize to the children the importance of sitting quietly and listening to the others as they talk about their chosen items. When all the suitable items have been put into the suitcase, talk about the ones left on the floor and ask why these items would be unsuitable to take on a summer holiday.

Give each child a copy of the photocopiable sheet. Talk about the pictures and help the children to cut them out. Invite them to put them into two piles, those which are suitable for a summer holiday and those which are not. Stick the holiday items onto the suitcase outline.

Support
Simply have a suitcase of items ready for a summer holiday and discuss the contents with the children without asking them to make choices.

Extension
Invite the children to colour in their photocopiable sheets before they cut them out and to go on to sort a selection of items into two suitcases, one for a cold winter holiday and one for a warm summer holiday.

Home links
Ask parents and carers to provide holiday items from home for the activity. Send home copies of the photocopiable sheet along with instructions so that carers and children can share the activity at home together.

Picnic time

What you need
Bread; various sandwich fillings such as egg, tuna, cheese, cucumber and salad; pictures of these fillings from magazines; knife; sliced bread; fruit; jugs; trays; orange juice; milk; water; plastic cups; paper plates; paper towels; picnic rugs; card.

What to do
Create a chart to show different types of sandwich fillings, using pictures of the fillings from magazines. Divide a large piece of landscape card into columns of squares and stick the sandwich filling pictures in the squares along the bottom. Write the children's names in the left-hand column of the chart.

Prepare the sandwich fillings and mix the drinks with the children. Ask each child to choose one of the sandwich fillings and help them to record their choice by putting a cross in the appropriate square on the chart. Count the number of each filling type and help the children to prepare the sandwiches, making the correct quantity according to the chart.

Prepare for the picnic, either indoors or outdoors, by placing the picnic rugs on the floor. Label each rug with a card depicting one of the drinks available.

Choose a child to give out plastic cups and offer the children a choice of cold drinks, such as milk, orange juice and water. Then encourage each child to find the rug corresponding to their choice of drink.

Put a jug of each type of drink on a tray and place the jugs on the corresponding blankets so that the children can pour out their own drinks. Finally, provide paper towels and give each child a plate containing their chosen sandwich.

Support
Have ready-made sandwiches for the children to choose from.

Extension
Create a 'Teddy Bears' Picnic' using plastic plates, cups and imitation food items. Invite each child to bring in from home a favourite teddy bear for the picnic.

Learning objective
To begin to recognize their own needs, feelings and views and to be sensitive to those of others.

Group size
Up to six children.

Home links
Have a nursery picnic outing, perhaps to a nearby park, and invite parents and carers to come with you. Invite a parent or carer from another culture to bring alternative examples of picnic food.

Planning a summer outing

What you need
Pictures, photographs and brochures of local places of interest.

Preparation
Gather together resources, if possible taking a small group of older children to a library and a travel agency to collect appropriate pictures and brochures.

What to do
The discussions before and after a visit are very important if a child is to benefit fully from the learning opportunities that the visit has to offer.

You will need, therefore, to plan these discussions fully.

Show the children the selection of pictures, photographs and brochures that you have collected. Talk to them about going on an outing together and ask them in turn to decide where they would like to go. Discuss the various options and decide which is the most popular suggestion. Talk about the chosen destination. Is it outdoors or indoors? What sort of clothing do the children think would be appropriate to wear? Talk about how the children would travel. Discuss various methods of transport and why each one is either appropriate or inappropriate.

Encourage the children to think about items that they might need to take with them. Will they need money? Might they need a packed lunch? Consider all the suggested items and decide on those which are necessary.

Stress any simple safety rules that will be needed, for example, proximity of water or busy roads.

Having discussed and prepared for the outing, set a date for it and invite parents and carers to join you so that you can enjoy an exciting visit together. On your return, plan time to talk to the children about it and to consider whether it was a success.

Support
Ensure that younger children are included in the discussions and encourage them to respond by considering appropriate vocabulary and questioning them effectively.

Extension
Take some photographs during the outing and use them as part of a home-made book, along with the children's drawings, written comments and other reminders of the day such as leaves, tickets and leaflets.

A fruity surprise

What you need
Selection of seasonal fresh fruit; large bowl; plastic knives; chopping boards; small plastic bowls; jug; fresh orange juice; spoons; the photocopiable sheet on page 70.

Preparation
Visit a market stall or supermarket with a small group of children to buy a selection of fruit. Make several copies of the photocopiable sheet onto card. Colour the pictures and laminate them, or cover them with sticky backed plastic, then cut the cards out.

What to do
Put one example of each of the fruit on the table and see how many the children can name. Discuss the different shapes and textures.

Provide each child with a small portion of each fruit to taste and invite them to describe it. Is it sweet or sour? Do they like or dislike the flavour? Ask them to describe how the fruit feels in their mouths. Is it crunchy or soft? So they like its texture?

Put all the fruit in the centre of the table and give each child a plastic bowl and a plastic knife. Ask them to choose something from the table to cut up on their chopping boards and put in their bowls. Supervise the children closely and offer hand-over-hand help with cutting where necessary. Give each child a portion of peeled orange to divide into segments. Throughout the activity, encourage the children to manage for themselves, offering help where necessary.

When all the fruit has been tasted and chopped into small pieces, invite each child to put the contents of their small bowl into one large bowl. Choose one child to pour fresh orange juice over the fruit salad and another to stir it. Ask the children to serve the fruit salad into small bowls, concentrating on serving equal portions and not spilling any, and to put a small plastic spoon into each bowl. Invite the rest of the nursery children to come and sit down so that those who prepared the fruit salad can serve them with a sample.

After eating the fruit salad, invite the children to play matching and sorting games using the fruit cards from the photocopiable sheet.

Support
Give the children the softer fruit to cut, such as bananas or strawberries.

Extension
Encourage the children to cut up the harder fruit, such as apples, into slices.

Outdoor code

Learning objective
To begin to understand what is right, what is wrong, and why.

Group size
Large group of children.

What you need
Coloured frieze paper; white sheets of paper; coloured paints; felt-tipped pens.

What to do
While playing outdoors, talk to the children about the importance of appropriate behaviour to ensure safety and to avoid the children being hurt. During circle time recall the discussion about behaviour and suggest that the children might like to create a group 'code of conduct' for outdoor play to display on the wall.

Discuss what the children consider to be right and wrong ways of behaving. Divide a large sheet of paper down the centre and write the headings 'right' and 'wrong' in the two sections. Invite the children to come out one by one and draw pictures of either appropriate or inappropriate actions. Write captions beneath the pictures summarizing what the children have said.

Read through the comments about inappropriate behaviour and decide which of these are most important to include in the 'code of conduct'. If important issues have not been considered, such as pushing somebody over or snatching equipment, then tactfully introduce these. Write the points out clearly or type them on a computer in large letters. Ensure that sentences are short and to the point, for example, 'We take turns on the slide', 'We never push one another' and so on. Space the sentences out and invite the children to draw a simple picture alongside each with felt-tipped pens.

Encourage the children to paint pictures of how to play safely outdoors. Display the paintings on the wall around the 'code of conduct'. Talk about each picture and write an associated safety rule underneath.

Support
Talk to the children about a specific aspect of behaviour using puppets to act out an inappropriate and an appropriate version of a situation.

Extension
Discuss the importance of road safety. Set up a role-play situation using home-made road signs and a crossing. Invite the local road safety officer to come and talk to the children. Discuss the consequences of not following simple rules when in traffic.

Home links
Ask parents and carers to create simple rules for the children to follow at home, such as keeping toys tidy and washing hands before meals. Type out the children's 'code of conduct' on A4 paper and send home a copy. Ask carers to reinforce the messages on it.

Caring for pets

What you need
Magazines with photographs of pets and wild animals; glue; sheets of sugar paper; crayons or paint; large needle; wool; a copy of the photocopiable sheet on page 71 for each child.

Preparation
Ask each child to bring in a photograph or a picture of their pet or of one of their favourite animals.

What to do
Explain how Buddha taught others about caring for all living things, emphasizing that there is a shared expectation across most cultures and beliefs to be sensitive to the needs of living things and to treat them with respect. Suggest that the children make a book about their pets and how they care for them.

Invite the children to draw or paint pictures of their pets or favourite animals. Mount each picture on a large sheet of sugar paper with a photograph of the relevant animal alongside. Encourage the children to help you make a front cover by creating a collage of pets and wild animals using pictures cut from magazines. Sew all the sheets together with a large needle and thick wool to form a book.

Talk about how important it is to look after animals and ask the children what they do to help look after their pet, for example, feeding, cleaning or walking. Encourage them to bring in items they use at home to care for their pets, such as food, feeding bowl, dog lead and bedding. Ask the children to help you display the home-made book and their pet items on a special 'Pet table'.

Give each child a set of cards made from the photocopiable sheet. Ask them to match the animals to their homes to make four pairs.

Support
Ask the children to draw simple pictures of their pets. Give them copies of the photocopiable sheet on paper and help them to draw lines between each animal and the correct home.

Extension
Encourage the children to write the names of their pets underneath their pictures, or scribe the names for them to copy.

Learning objective
To have a developing awareness of the needs and feelings of animals and show a sense of responsibility in caring for them.

Group size
Large group for discussion; up to ten children for the activity.

Home links
Ask parents and carers to take their children to a pet shop to buy something for their pets or to look at the variety of things that can be used to care for pets.

That's magic!

Learning objective
To become aware of their own feelings and emotions.

Group size
Up to 12 children.

What you need

Long chiffon scarves or light fabric; appropriate music, such as 'Dance of the Sugar Plum Fairy' from *The Nutcracker* by Tchaikovsky or 'Dance of the Elves' from *A Midsummer Night's Dream* by Mendelssohn.

What to do

Talk to the children about Midsummer's Day and explain to them that this is a time when mythical characters, traditionally fairies and witches, are believed to appear. If you prefer not to introduce witches into the activity, simply concentrate on fairies. Create props for fairies using long pieces of chiffon or net with loops to hook over the children's wrists, and add streamers of tissue to kitchen-roll tubes for those who wish to be magical creatures.

Ask the children what they think fairies look like and explain to them that fairies are 'make-believe', which means that they do not really exist. Suggest to the children that they might like to pretend to be fairies or magical woodland creatures and make up their own dances.

Introduce some appropriate music (see 'What you need') and begin by asking the children to sit or lie quietly on the floor and close their eyes as they listen. Explain that the music was especially composed so that ballet dancers could pretend to be fairies or elves. Talk about how fairies might move. Will they move quickly and lightly, or plod around heavily and slowly? Play the music again and ask the children to listen to what they think the music is telling them as they move around the room.

Display the props so that the children can easily choose what they would like to use during their dance. Ask them to choose something to wave as they move about to create the illusion of floating or flying.

Introduce some more powerful music as a contrast to the light fairy music, for example, *The Sorcerer's Apprentice* by Dukas or *Danse Macabre* by Saint-Saëns. Talk about how the music makes the children feel, but be careful not to include any music which might make the children feel overwhelmed.

Support

Invite the children to concentrate on moving to just one piece of music.

Extension

Encourage the children to listen to contrasting music and to choose the one which they feel is the most appropriate.

Home links
Invite parents and carers to the setting to watch their children dance.

Textured treasures

What you need
Photograph frame; one of your family pictures; three different-coloured paints; a variety of small-grain products in a variety of textures, such as sand, rice, glitter, salt, sugar, tea leaves, washing powder and sawdust; glitter; washing powder; paintbrushes; A4 card; A5 paper; scissors; glue; camera.

Preparation
Mix some of the dry materials into each of the different colours of paint so that each colour is a different texture.

What to do
Talk to the children about Father's Day and explain to them how important it is to thank the people who are kind to them and take care of them.

Show the children a family photograph in a frame and suggest that they make their own photograph frames as presents for a father, male carer or relative. Remain sensitive to individual circumstances.

Take a photograph of each child with the nursery camera or ask the children to draw portraits of themselves on A5 pieces of paper. Prepare the frames by giving each child an A4 piece of card and asking them to paint patterns on the card using their choice of the textured paints. When the paint has dried, encourage the children to feel their pictures and describe the different textures. Ask them, 'Which side of the card feels rough?' and invite them to

compare this rough surface with the smooth surface on the other side.

Cut out a square in the middle of each piece of card, making sure the cut-out square is a bit smaller than the child's photograph or drawing. Glue around the edges of the photograph or drawing and stick it to the frame.

Finally, glue another piece of A4 card to the picture and frame as backing.

Support
Offer close supervision to the children when they are painting their frames. Write the children's names under their pictures for them.

Extension
Invite the children to try mixing their own textured paint. Let them write their own names under their pictures.

Learning objective
To form good relationships with adults and show sensitivity to others.

Group size
Up to six children.

Home links
Invite a father or male carer to come to your setting and read a story to the children.

Friezing flames

What you need
Paper plates; coloured paints; collage materials; glue; red, orange and yellow tissue paper and paint; sheets of white paper; coloured frieze paper; pieces of sponge cut into flame shapes.

What to do
Talk to the children about the Christian festival of Pentecost and explain to them how the Holy Spirit came down to the disciples, giving them the courage

and strength to continue Jesus' work of teaching and caring for others. Tell the children how the presence of the Holy Spirit was described as being a flame above the head of each disciple. Suggest that the children make a picture of this event.

Ask each child to create a smiling face on a paper plate by using paints and collage materials. Put a large piece of coloured frieze paper onto the floor and attach the paper plates in a row towards the bottom of it. Explain that these are the disciples.

Encourage the children to paint flames above the disciples' heads with yellow, orange and red paint. As they paint, emphasize the dangers of fire.

Once the paint is dry, invite the children to stick strips of tissue paper above the plates to create a more textured flame effect. Then ask them to print a border using the pieces of sponge cut into flame shapes and dipped into red, yellow or orange paint. Attach the frieze to the wall.

Tell the children about how Jesus cared for others and ask them to think about ways in which they can be kind to their friends and families. Write their ideas onto pieces of white paper and attach these to the frieze above and in between the flames. Create a caption in large letters saying 'We are kind to each other' and place this underneath the frieze title 'Pentecost'.

Support
Help the children by painting the flame shapes yourself, encouraging them to stick torn-up tissue on top of them.

Extension
Invite the children to write out their ideas for how to be kind to others themselves, or scribe the words for them to copy.

Dragon drama

What you need
Large cardboard box; large sheets of card or cardboard boxes opened out; red foil; tissue paper; recycled materials; glue; nine chairs; sticky tape; green paint; broom handles; percussion instruments; the photocopiable sheet on page 72.

What to do
Talk to the children about how the Chinese remember Ch'u Yuan who drowned himself to try and help his people. To save his body from the dragons and demons, the people took a boat into the lake and made loud noises and threw rice wrapped in bamboo leaves to keep the dragons at bay. Sing the 'Dragon drama' song with the children and make up actions. Suggest that the children make their own dragon boat and use it to act out the story.

Begin by making the dragon's head from a cardboard box. Use recycled items for the features, for example, an egg-box mouth and yoghurt-pot eyes.

Ask the children to glue on the features and paint the finished head green. Use red foil to create 'flames' coming from the dragon's mouth. Attach the finished dragon's head to a chair with sticky tape and place four pairs of chairs in a row. Ask the children to paint large sheets of card with green paint and tape the card around the outside of the chairs to form a 'boat'. Make eight oars from broom handles and sheets of card.

Invite the children to sit in the boat and row. Encourage them to work together, pulling forward and backward at the same time. Make loud noises using percussion instruments and by shouting to frighten away the dragons.

Support
Ensure that the children are not disconcerted by the noise levels. Help them to hold the oars and row.

Extension
Ask the children to help you make up additional verses for the song.

Learning objective
To be confident to try new activities, initiate ideas and speak in front of a group.

Group size
Up to 12 children.

Doctor Foster

What you need
Waterproof raincoat and wellington boots for each child; umbrellas or waterproof hats; large circles of blue fabric; an enlarged copy of the photocopiable sheet on page 73.

Preparation
Prepare a puddle from a large sheet of blue fabric for each child in the group.

What to do
Talk about the old belief that if it rains on St Swithun's Day then it is likely to rain for the next 40 days. Say the rhyme on the photocopiable sheet with the children. Ask them what clothing they think would be suitable to wear outside in the rain. Talk about outdoor clothing and how important it is to wear waterproof clothes when it is raining, or when it is likely to rain.

Place the 'puddles' on the floor in an open area. Let the children put on their waterproof clothing and give each child a small umbrella or a waterproof hat to wear. Explain that as you say the rhyme together again, they should walk around the room in their waterproof clothing, avoiding the puddles on the floor. At the end of the rhyme, ask the children to find a puddle, jump onto it and sit down, pretending to be Doctor Foster. Encourage the children to take turns to say the rhyme while others mime the actions.

Support
Offer plenty of help to the children in putting on outdoor clothing.

Extension
Ask the children to think of reasons why rain is important.

Home links
Ask parents and carers to provide waterproof clothing and umbrellas. Give the children copies of the photocopiable sheet to learn at home.

Swing high, swing low

Learning objective
To begin to understand that people have different views, cultures and beliefs, which need to be treated with respect.

Group size
Up to six children.

What you need
Favourite nursery doll; long wide ribbons or strips of fabric; collage materials such as foil, tissue paper, glitter, tinsel and sweet papers; cereal box; scissors; glue; coloured paints; two sturdy wooden chairs.

What to do
Begin by explaining to the children that Janamashtami is a Hindu festival during which Hindus celebrate the birth of Krishna. They make a decorated swing in which they place either a picture or a statue of the infant Krishna and, as they walk past the swing, they take turns to push it gently. Suggest that the children make a decorated swing for their favourite nursery doll, using recycled materials and collage scraps.

Cut the fabric or ribbon into long strips and cut the front side off a cereal box to create a shallow container. Invite the children to decorate the strips of fabric using colourful collage materials and glue. Wind the decorated strips around each chair until both are covered and place the chairs back to back, leaving a gap in between, big enough for the swing.

Ask the children to paint and decorate the outside of the cereal box so that it can be used for the seat of the swing. Put a piece of soft fabric into the box for the doll to sit on.

Attach a strip of the decorated fabric to each corner of the box and then tie two strips to the top of one chair and two strips to the other, to create a swing. Encourage the children to take turns to push the nursery doll gently on the swing.

Support
Offer plenty of assistance to the children in decorating the material strips and the box.

Extension
Talk with the children about how Hindus washed the statue of Krishna with ghee, yoghurt, milk and honey. Make a similar mixture with the children, omitting the ghee. Encourage them to taste the mixture and to describe its taste. Ask questions such as, 'Is it sweet?', 'Do you like the taste?' and so on. (Before starting this activity, remember to check for allergies and dietary requirements.)

Home links
Invite a parent or carer with a baby to come and talk to the children about the birth of the baby and family celebrations. Ask each child to bring in a favourite doll from home to push on the swing.

Elegant elephants

What you need
A picture of Ganesh; paper plates; coloured Cellophane; sticky tape; newspaper; glue; string; grey paint; card; scissors; grey or black socks; glitter; sequins.

What to do
Begin by talking to the children about how Hindus celebrate the birthday of Ganesh, the elephant-headed god of wisdom and prosperity. Look at a picture of the god and ask the children to imagine how they would manage with an elephant's trunk instead of a nose. Suggest that they make elephant-head masks to wear.

Cut out some ear and tusk shapes from card. Show the children how to tear the newspaper into short strips and to glue this randomly onto two ear shapes and a paper plate to represent the rough texture of elephant skin.

Secure the ears onto either side of the paper plate using glue or sticky tape, and paint the whole mask grey. Add the card tusks and cut two holes for the eyes and a small hole for the trunk. Help each child to push a sock through the centre hole to form a trunk. Secure the sock to the back of the plate with sticky tape.

Encourage the children to decorate the mask by blobbing it with glue and scattering sequins and glitter over it. Shake the mask to remove any sequins and glitter that have not stuck. Make a head-dress from a piece of coloured Cellophane glued to the plate. Attach string to the sides of the mask for fastening and help each child to put their mask on.

Support
Provide plenty of assistance to the children with cutting and sticking. Scatter sequins and glitter with them so that they can copy your action.

Extension
Give the children a range of collage materials and encourage them to create other animal masks, such as lions, cats, dogs and pigs, in their own designs.

Autumn collage

What you need
A selection of autumn fruit; glue and spreaders; small pots; thick card in autumn colours; black sugar paper; seaside buckets; books about autumn; magnifying glasses; brown fabric; paint; extra adult support.

Preparation
Cut the card into large leaf shapes and prepare a display board with a bare tree outline made from black sugar paper in the centre.

What to do
Take the children on an autumn walk, perhaps to a local park. Ask them to pick up autumn items, such as fallen leaves, twigs, pine-cones and acorns. Give the children a bucket each in which to make their collection.

Back indoors, empty the contents of the buckets onto a table and talk about them. What do they feel and smell like? Help the children to sort the items, for example, into piles of leaves, conkers or twigs. Look at reference books and see if you can identify all of the items.

Ask each child to choose a card 'leaf' and provide individual pots of PVA glue and spreaders. Demonstrate how to

stick different items from the selection onto a leaf and then let the children choose freely to create their own leaf collage. Once dry, staple the finished leaves along the bottom of the display board below the tree outline. Encourage the children to paint pictures of themselves, cut them out and glue them to the display. Entitle the picture 'Our autumn walk'.

Stand a table in front of the display and cover it in a brown cloth. Arrange the remaining autumn collection on the table for free exploration, along with the autumn fruit, appropriate books, magnifying glasses and labels.

Support
Encourage older children or adults to hold the hands of younger children and help them to find suitable items during the walk.

Extension
Make a small-world autumn scene. Half-fill a sand tray with soil. Stick twigs into the soil to represent bare trees and scatter small brown leaves over the surface. Make a path using pebbles. Put small-world figures and suitable small-world animals on the path.

Learning objective
To be able to select from a range of resources for a chosen task.

Group size
Up to six children.

Home links
Ask parents and carers to supply autumn collage materials from their gardens or to take their children for a walk to collect them.

Leaf pictures

What you need
A selection of large leaves from trees such as sycamores and horse chestnuts; white paper cut into large leaf shapes; coloured wax crayons; coloured thick paint; sponges; shallow containers; paintbrushes.

What to do
Take the children for a walk to collect leaves and dry them out indoors, or ask carers and staff to bring a selection of

leaves to your setting. Talk about the leaves in the collection and explain to the children that you are going to use them to make leaf pictures to display on one of the walls.

Arrange a selection of real leaves on a table along with the large white paper leaves and thick crayons, and demonstrate how to make a leaf rubbing by placing a leaf under the paper and rubbing the length of a crayon across the top of it. Encourage each child to make their own leaf rubbing and, once they have completed one, ask them to swap their leaf with a friend to create another

rubbing, using a different-coloured crayon. Compare all the leaf rubbings and talk about the different patterns, shapes and colours used.

Place shallow trays filled with different-coloured thick paint in the centre of another table. Concentrate on autumn colours, or use a wider range to encourage more creative expression.

Show the children how to make leaf prints by painting one side of a leaf and carefully pressing it down onto a large paper leaf. Provide a selection of leaves and ask the children to make their own leaf-print pictures. Supply sponges with each colour to wipe off excess paint. Once the children have made their rubbings using one method, let the groups swap tables so that they try the other technique. Mount the rubbings and prints on contrasting paper and display them together on the wall. Talk about the differences between the wax and paint pictures. Which pictures show the leaf patterns more clearly?

Support
Help each child with their wax rubbing by holding the paper in place for them as they rub with the crayon.

Extension
Talk about how some trees lose their leaves in autumn while others remain green all year round. Examine some evergreen branches and make observational drawings.

Autumn dance

Learning objective
To dress and undress
independently.

Group size
Large group.

What you need
A tape recorder or CD player;
appropriate 'autumn' music such as
Vivaldi's *The Four Seasons*, 'Autumn'
movement; selection of leaves.

What to do
Arrange to have a pile of leaves available
for outdoor play. Throw them in the air
and see how they float to the ground,
then take the children to observe some
branches swaying in the wind.

Back indoors remind the children of
their outdoor activities with leaves and
branches. Discuss how the leaves moved
as they fell to the ground and how the
branches waved in the wind. Play the
chosen music to the children and ask
them to close their eyes and imagine
leaves and branches floating and
swaying. Tell the children to take off
their shoes and socks and to remove
any outer garments, such as jumpers
and cardigans, and to put them all in a
neat pile at the side of the room. Ask
older children to help their younger
friends. Play the music again and
suggest to the children that they move
like leaves or branches.

Play the music a third time and let
the children decide whether they would
like to be leaves or branches. Invite the
'branches' to stand in the centre of the
room 'swaying in the wind' while the
'leaves' skip and dance in between
them before eventually falling to the
ground. Swap roles and repeat the
dance. At the end of the activity, ask
the children to find their own clothes,
shoes and socks and put them on again.

Support
Offer assistance to the children in
taking off and putting on garments.

Extension
Talk about clothes worn during different
seasons of the year. Have two sets of
items prepared, one set of summer
accessories and one set of winter
accessories. Include items such as hats,
sun-glasses, gloves, a scarf, sandals and
boots. Ask two older children to put the
things on and time them to see
whether it takes longer to put on the
summer or winter items. Discuss reasons
for your findings. Play a team game
taking turns to put on the sets of things.

Home links
Ask parents and
carers to help their
children learn to dress
themselves for
outdoor play, change
their shoes and
recognize the name
labels on their clothes.

The little red hen

What you need
Paper plates; collage materials; brown paint; thick card; elastic; wheat seeds or something similar such as buttons or beads; small cardboard boxes; copy of *The Little Red Hen* (traditional).

Preparation
Make some animal masks for a pig, cat, dog and hen using thick card and collage materials. Make ears on head-bands and a beak on elastic to offer as an alternative for children who do not like to wear masks. Paint small cardboard boxes with brown paint to represent the loaves of bread, or make some with salt dough.

What to do
Talk to the children about how wheat is grown to make bread, and explain that the beginning of autumn is when the crops are harvested.

Read *The Little Red Hen* to the children and discuss the behaviour of the hen and the other animals in the story. Dramatize the story with some of the children using the props and taking turns to play the different animal characters in the story while the rest of the group watches.

Encourage the children to talk about the behaviour of the cat, the rat and the pig. What do they think it means to be lazy? Do the children think the animals were lazy? Do they think the Little Red Hen should have shared the bread with the other animals? If not, why not? Do the children think that the animals could change their ways?

Talk about appropriate group behaviour in the nursery. Ask the children to think of times at nursery when they share something with friends, such as a snack or piece of construction equipment. How would the children feel if someone ate all of the morning snack or did not share the equipment?

In circle time, play turn-taking games and share out snacks.

Support
Read the story to small groups of children, encouraging them to join in on repeated lines. Ask them to point out the different characters.

Extension
Encourage the children to make suggestions for appropriate behaviour, and involve them in the preparation of a chart showing a code of behaviour for your setting. Ask the children to paint pictures for each statement to display beside the chart.

Fun with apples

What you need
A selection of different apples including eating and cooking apples with a variety of skin colours; magnifying glasses; chopping board; fairly blunt knife; two bowls; red and green colouring materials; a copy of the photocopiable sheet on page 74 for each child.

Preparation
Take a small group of children to buy as wide a selection of apples as possible and ask parents and carers to send in donations. Cut up some of the apples into quarters before the activity.

What to do
Arrange examples of each of the different varieties of apples in the middle of a table for the children to examine. Ask each child to choose an apple and to describe how it feels and smells. Is it hard or soft, rough or smooth, shiny or dull, warm or cold? Are any of the apples bruised? Explain how apples become bruised when they fall to the ground. Have any of the children ever been bruised after a fall, on their knees, for example? Ask each child to describe the colour of the apple skin. Is it the same all over?

Cut an apple in half and look at the centre. Take out some pips and let the children examine them with magnifying glasses. Explain that these are the seeds of the apple and reserve some to plant in pots later.

Let each child have a turn at cutting the apple quarters into small pieces as you supervise them hand-over-hand. Put the pieces into two bowls. At snack time, choose two children to give out the apple pieces to the rest of the children. Ask them to describe the taste and texture of their apple pieces. Are they sweet or sour, crunchy or soft? Why texture do the children prefer?

Support
To make cutting easier, peel the apple portions for the children. Give them copies of the photocopiable sheet and ask them to colour the apples in reds and greens.

Extension
Give the children copies of the photocopiable sheet and encourage them to work in pairs, taking turns to number or initial each apple in the picture. Ask each child to count how many apples they have coloured in or written their initials on. Is it the same number as their partner's?

Learning objective
To continue to be interested, excited and motivated to learn.

Group size
Up to six children.

Home links
Ask parents and carers to provide apples for the activity. Invite them to the setting to help you carry out cooking activities with the children, following simple apple recipes.

All aglow

What you need

A selection of candles, lamps and torches; coloured paint and crayons; paper; kitchen-roll tubes; glue; yellow Cellophane; glitter; sequins; a copy of the photocopiable sheet on page 75 for each child.

What to do

Discuss the lengthening days of autumn and the difference between light and dark. Talk about how summer evenings are light whereas in autumn it becomes dark early. Ask the children to think of how they light up a dark room at home and how streets are lit at night.

Make the room as dark as possible by turning off any lights and pulling blinds or curtains. Sit together in a group and talk about how difficult it is to see objects clearly around the room now that it is dark. Try different ways of lighting the room, such as switching on the main light, using a small lamp, lighting a large candle, lighting a small birthday-cake candle or shining a torch. Introduce unusual variations, such as a fibre optic or lava lamp. Ensure that the children are at a safe distance when lighting candles and emphasize the dangers of naked flames.

Encourage the children to discuss the different types of lighting and to think

about which one they liked best and which one produced the most light in the room.

Use a torch to highlight certain objects. Explain the importance of candles in the days before electricity and make models of candles with the children using kitchen-roll tubes. Ask each child to paint a tube and decorate it with glitter and sequins before sticking a yellow Cellophane flame to the top. Display your selection of real candles alongside the children's model candles. Ask the children to draw and paint pictures of candles to display on the wall behind.

Give each child a copy of the photocopiable sheet and use it to discuss the different types of lighting. Encourage the children to offer their own suggestions of other forms of lighting and to draw another kind of light in the blank square.

Support

Draw the faint outline of a street lamp in the final box on the photocopiable sheet for the children to colour in.

Extension

Ask the children to draw any more sources of light that they can think of on the back of the photocopiable sheet.

Open house!

What you need
Two cups each of self-raising flour, castor sugar and margarine; two eggs; large mixing bowl; a small plastic tub for each child; teaspoons; paper cake-cases; two tablespoons of chocolate powder; fruit juices; paper plates; napkins; plastic cups; coloured table-cloth.

What to do
Talk to the children about the names they have for their grandparents or

special older relatives and encourage each child to tell the rest of the group about one of them. Suggest to the children that they organize an open day for grandparents and other older friends on Grandparent's Day. Consider the type of food grandparents might enjoy and talk about whether the children could prepare it themselves.

Make some cakes for the special day. Choose different children to mix the sugar and margarine together in a large bowl, add the two beaten eggs and mix in the flour (always wash hands after handling raw eggs). Encourage the children to take turns to stir the mixture in the large bowl. Give each child a portion of the mixture in a small plastic tub and ask them to fill their cake cases. Repeat the recipe with another group of children, this time adding two tablespoons of chocolate powder to make some chocolate cakes. Bake the cakes in a moderate oven for 12–15 minutes and allow them to cool in a safe place.

Mix some fruit juices for the children and their guests. Display the cakes on a table decorated with a colourful table-cloth and a vase of flowers. Encourage the children to help with serving by putting cakes onto paper plates along with napkins.

Ask each child to pick a favourite song to sing to the elderly guests. Let them decide whether they would like to sing the song alone or with the other children in the group.

Support
Give the children only the simpler tasks such as spooning out the finished mixture into the cake cases.

Extension
Let the children make invitations to give out beforehand and place cards with the names of the guests on them.

Learning objective
To be confident to try new activities, initiate ideas and speak in front of a group.

Group size
Up to six children.

Home links
Invite parents and carers to help with the cake-making. Send home an invitation with each child for a chosen relative or friend.

Sound the horn!

What you need
Large sheets of thick paper; thin card; cardboard tubes; newspaper; cassette tape or CD; music system; scissors.

What to do
Explain how Jewish New Year is called 'Rosh Hashana' and how at this time a ram's horn, or 'shofar', is blown to call people to prayer. Establish what the

children understand 'praying' to mean. Arrange the resources on a table and ask the children to try to make cone-shaped horns with the different-sized pieces of thick paper and thin card. Provide different lengths of cardboard tubing as ready-made horns. Ask the children to shout through their home-made horns and the tubes and decide which one produces the loudest noise. Try turning the cones around and shouting through the widest end. Does this alter the volume of the sound? Discuss how we manage to hear the

different sounds and look closely at one another's ears.

Explain that some people cannot hear things clearly. To demonstrate this, play a favourite tape or CD of music for the children at a normal volume. Next, turn the volume down slightly, explaining that this is how some people hear the music. Finally, turn the volume off and explain that people who are deaf cannot hear at all. Talk about hearing aids and how they help people who have hearing difficulties. Discuss the problems associated with hearing loss, such as not being able to hear other people talking, and consider how deaf people communicate in other ways, such as sign language. Try communicating using simple gestures, such as nodding and waving. Can the children understand what you mean? Learn a favourite rhyme using sign language or appropriate actions.

Support
Provide ready-made cones and tubes for the children to explore rather than asking them to create their own.

Extension
Provide the children with information books about musical instruments and ask them to find pictures of instruments that are played by blowing. Explain that they are called wind instruments. Ask the children to paint their tubes and horns to look like a chosen wind instrument.

Learning objective
To have a developing awareness of the needs of others.

Group size
Up to six children.

Home links
Invite a relative of one of the children or someone from the community with hearing difficulties to talk to the group about their problems. Invite a parent or carer to play a wind instrument.

Harvest basket

What you need
Shoeboxes; strips of thick card; coloured tissue paper; wrapping paper in autumn colours; cling film; sticky tape; card; felt-tipped pens; glue; Cellophane; artificial-grass table covering; a copy of the photocopiable sheet on page 76 for each child.

Preparation
Ask the children to bring in a selection of fresh, tinned and packet foods from home.

What to do
Begin by talking about the significance of harvest time and about the needs of elderly people. Explain to the children that the Harvest Festival is a time for giving thanks to God through prayers and hymns in church for the gift of fruit and vegetables grown during the year. Talk about how we give harvest baskets to show people that we are thinking of them.

Give each child a copy of the photocopiable sheet and ask them to choose their favourite fruit and vegetables from the selection. Then help them to cut these out and to stick them onto the harvest basket at the top of the sheet.

Suggest to the children that they might like to make a harvest gift for a special elderly relative or friend. Encourage each child to tell you and the rest of the group why their chosen relative or friend is so special to them.

Give each child a shoebox and help them to cover it with the wrapping paper of their choice. Make a handle from a strip of card and stick it to each side of the box with sticky tape. Line the box with coloured tissue paper and sort the harvest gifts brought by the children into separate piles, such as fresh fruit, vegetables, tins and packets. Invite each child to choose something from each pile of food to put into their box, continuing until they have filled it. Write the name of the recipient of the box on a card and put it on top of the contents. Cover the box with Cellophane. Arrange all the boxes on a table covered with artificial grass.

Invite the relatives and friends to a harvest morning and let the children sing their favourite songs to them before giving out the boxes.

Support
Help the children to cover their boxes and encourage them to name the fruit and vegetables.

Extension
Take a group of children on a visit to a residential home for the elderly with harvest gifts of fruit. Ensure that there are enough baskets so that the children can give one to each resident. Encourage the children to sing some seasonal songs to the residents.

Learning objective
To form good relationships with people of all ages.

Group size
Small groups of up to six children with an adult.

Home links
Send home a request for items for harvest gifts and the name of an elderly relative to receive one of the boxes made by the children. Give the children copies of the photocopiable sheet to complete at home with their parents or carers.

Let's be happy!

What you need
Coloured frieze paper; white paper; coloured paints; paintbrushes; story-book.

What to do
Explain to the children that Yom Kippur is the holiest day of the year in the Jewish calendar and that it is a time when Jewish families say sorry to each other for anything they have done that was upsetting.

Discuss a range of emotions with the children, including feeling scared, worried, surprised, angry, happy and sad. Ask each child to think of times when they feel happy and times when they feel sad. Read an appropriate story to extend the discussion or to encourage the children to explore their own feelings, for example, *Dogger* by Shirley Hughes (Red Fox). Can the children suggest kind actions that can be found in the story?

Encourage each child to tell the rest of the group about a time when they were feeling very sad and to describe what made them feel happy again. Was it the action of another person? If so, what did this person do to make them feel happier?

Ask the children to think about ways that they can cheer people up, and encourage them to paint a 'happy' picture. Then tell them that you are going to make a wall display contrasting their ideas about what makes them happy and what makes them sad.

Divide the display area into two sections of frieze paper, using a bright colour for happiness and a dull colour for sadness, and attach the children's work to the 'happy' side. Make simple captions for each picture, emphasizing the action that resulted in happiness, and stick these alongside. Ask the children to paint pictures of actions by others that make them feel sad and hang these on the other half of the display board with appropriate captions.

Support
During the discussion about emotions with the children, just concentrate on happiness and sadness.

Extension
Encourage the children to demonstrate caring by taking turns to serve drinks and food to one another at snack time.

! Party time

Learning objective
To develop a sense of community, understanding that people have different views, needs, cultures and beliefs.

Group size
Six children to prepare the raita; the whole group for the party.

What you need
Indian food such as cooked rice, poppadoms, chapattis and samosas; natural yoghurt; cucumber; mint sauce; strips of white paper; coloured paint; sticky tape; dressing-up clothes; sheets of coloured material.

What to do
Explain that Divali, the Hindu New Year festival, is an important time for family parties and community celebrations. Talk about parties and celebrations that the children have been to. Plan a nursery Divali party together, listing the types of Indian food to be sampled and favourite games to be played. Make garlands for party decorations by asking the children to paint coloured patterns onto strips of white paper and linking the strips with sticky tape to form colourful chains. Look at pictures of Indian clothing and make saris out of sheets of colourful material.

Make some cucumber raita with the children. Chop half a cucumber into small pieces and add it to a large carton of yoghurt along with a dessertspoon of mint sauce or some chopped mint. Set out the food samples, including the raita, onto a table and ask the children to sample them. Encourage them to describe the different tastes. Do they like or dislike the flavours?

Talk about how girls decorate their hands with mendhi patterns and let them try to copy some of the designs onto their own hands using face-paints. Suggest that the children wear dressing-up clothes from the home corner for the party (ensure that you include some pieces of fabric to create saris). Play Indian music and ask the children to imagine how people would move to the music. Encourage them to dance and play some favourite party games before sitting down for the party food.

Support
Help the children to stick their painted strips together for the garlands and paint their hands for them.

Extension
Invite the children to work in pairs to make up routines to the music and perform them to the rest of the group.

Home links
Send home a sheet of recipes for Indian food, such as raita and samosas. Make samosas with the children so that they can take a sample home.

Highland fling!

Learning objective
To respond to
significant
experiences with a
range of feelings.

Group size
12 children.

What you need
Tapes of Scottish music, such as
bagpipe tunes, highland dance music
and folk music; Scottish items for a
display.

What to do
Talk about St Andrew's Day with the
children and tell them that you are
going to make a display about
Scotland. Find out about the possibility
of someone coming to play bagpipes to
the children or a local Scottish dancing
class coming to dance.

Ask the children to sit quietly and
listen to the different examples of
Scottish music. Encourage them to talk
about and compare each piece. Invite
each child to tell the rest of the group
what they thought of the music and
how it made them feel. Did they like
the music? Did it make them feel like
dancing, or sitting quietly to listen?
Play each piece of music again and
encourage the children to move in
time to it.

Ideally, show the children a video of
dancing or of some Scottish country
dancers and then encourage them to
hold hands with a partner and skip

around the room to some traditional
Scottish dance music.

Finally, divide the children into two
groups, then the first group into pairs.
Show them how to link hands in the air
with their partners and ask the other
group to skip underneath the linked
'arches'. Change positions and repeat
the dance.

Support
Encourage older children to hold hands
with younger friends for the dancing.

Extension
Make bagpipes with the children using
kitchen-roll tubes, scrap material and
paints. Cut scraps of plain material into
large circle shapes. Give a circle to each
child and demonstrate how to decorate
it with 'tartan' patterns by painting
coloured lines, first down the material
and then across. Press holes in the
kitchen-roll tubes using a sharp pencil
and ask each child to paint or decorate
their tube. Form a bag shape with the
'tartan' material and attach it to the
tube by gathering together the edge of
the circle and securing it with an elastic
band to one end of the tube.

Home links
Invite parents and
carers to watch their
children's dancing
and to share some
shortbread made by
the group. Ask carers
to provide items for
the 'Scottish' display,
such as a tartan rug,
pictures of Scotland
or some shortbread,
and to dress their
children in kilts for the
dance performance if
they have them.

Hang up the kindness

What you need
Washing line; pegs; strips of paper; felt-tipped pens.

What to do
Talk to the children about Guru Nanak, the founder of the Sikh faith, explaining that he was kind and brought happiness into people's lives. Establish what the children understand by kindness.

At the end of a circle-time session, ask the children to think of a time when they have been kind to someone else. Encourage each child to stand up and talk to the others about their action. When everybody has spoken, join hands in the circle to form a 'ring of kindness' and talk about the importance of being kind to each other.

Now tell the group that you are going to make a 'kindness line'. Hang the washing line across a corner of the room or along the wall at child height. Write down the children's kind deeds on strips of paper and let the children peg them to the line. At the end of the session, read the strips together and then let the children take them home.

Have regular 'kindness line' days and encourage the children to come and tell you about the kind deeds of other people rather than their own. Keep a note of names to ensure that all children are included and encouraged to consider their actions.

Support
Give examples to help the children think of a time when they have been kind, such as when they let friends borrow favourite toys.

Extension
Ask the children to draw or paint a picture about how they have been kind to others. Mount the pictures on coloured frieze paper and attach them to the wall to form a large circle.

Write simple captions to put beside each child's picture describing the child's action, then make a large caption 'Our ring of kindness' to display above the frieze.

Encourage the children to paint pictures of their special friends in your group, and make another circle with these pictures and entitle it 'Our ring of friendship'.

Learning objective
To consider the consequences of words and actions for themselves and others.

Group size
Whole group.

Home links
Invite a family member or friend who works as a carer, or volunteers for charity work, to come and talk to the children about how they help others.

Learning objective
To develop a sense of community and belonging.

Group size
Up to six children.

Little stars

What you need
Pictures of the Star of David; collage printing materials such as sponges, potatoes and corrugated cardboard; plastic triangles; selection of coloured paints; paper; cardboard; scissors; safety-pins; sticky tape.

What to do
Talk about the festival of Hanukkah and explain how important the Star of

David is to Jewish People. Look at pictures of the Star and experiment with two plastic triangles to see if the children can form a Star of David by overlapping them. Suggest that the children might like to try printing with or drawing around the triangles to see if they can make their own Stars of David on paper.

Provide printing materials, such as sponge, corrugated cardboard or potatoes, already cut into star shapes and ask the children to print with them using the thick coloured paints provided. Encourage them to print one triangle on top of the other to form the six-pointed Star of David.

Talk about the different colours chosen by the children for their star pictures. Have some children chosen only one colour for their printed picture? Explain to the children how colours and symbols are often used to give a sense of belonging to a group. If the children wear a uniform, such as a nursery sweatshirt, use this as an example. Ask if anybody has an older brother or sister who wears a uniform for school. Talk about how some adults have to wear special uniforms at work for safety, such as fire officers. Discuss what would happen if certain people did not wear a uniform. What would happen if police officers wore ordinary clothes?

Invite the children to help you create a nursery logo, such as a star-shaped badge made from cardboard. Ask them to choose a favourite colour for the badge, then agree on the most popular colour and help each child to paint their cardboard badge. Secure a safety-pin to the back with sticky tape. If you have a nursery grouping system, invite the children to create a different design or use a different colour for each group.

Support
Demonstrate to the children how to overlap the triangle prints to form stars and provide as much help as necessary.

Extension
Encourage the children to try drawing star shapes without a guide. Show them how to draw and overlap two separate triangles to create a Star of David.

Day and night

What you need
A4 card; large sheet of yellow card; scissors; felt-tipped pens; two copies of the photocopiable sheet on page 77.

Preparation
Invite the children to help you prepare the picture cards for the activity. Ask them to colour in two copies of the photocopiable sheet, and stick them onto strong card. Then help the children to cut out the pictures. Make extra copies if you are working with a larger group. Finally, prepare a large

sun shape and a large moon shape from yellow card.

What to do
Ask the children to sit in a circle and begin by talking about the differences between day and night. Discuss the children's night-time routines. What do they do before going to bed? Do they

brush their teeth? Do they prepare their clothes for the next day? Do their parents or carers read them a story?

Show the children the prepared picture cards of things seen during the day and those seen during the night and suggest that they play a game with them. Place the card sun and moon on the floor in the centre of the circle and spread the picture cards face down around them.

Invite each child in turn to choose a card and look at the picture. Ask them to decide whether to put the card onto the sun or the moon according to whether the item is seen in the daytime or at night.

Discuss each child's choice with the other children in the group. Does everyone agree with the individual choices made? Repeat the exercise once more so that all the cards are turned over.

Support
Play a guessing game with the children, asking them to guess which items associated with night-time you have in your bag. Include objects such as a toothbrush, towel, pyjamas, slippers, teddy bear or doll, book and night light.

Extension
Ask the children to make pictorial charts of noises that might be heard outside in the daytime. Take them outside and ask them to make a tick in the correct column each time a specific noise is heard, for example, a dog, a bird, a passer-by and so on. Return to the setting to compare your results.

Learning objective
To maintain attention, concentrate and sit quietly when appropriate.

Group size
Five children.

Home links
Send home copies of the photocopiable sheet and instructions so that parents and carers can play the game with their children.

Keeping warm!

What you need
Baking potatoes (half of them pre-cooked); tin foil; fillings such as baked beans, tuna and cheese; salad cream; chives; large mixing bowl; wooden spoon; teaspoons; forks; recipe books; plates; small bowls.

What to do
Talk to the children about cold weather and how eating hot food can help them to feel warm. Ask the children about their favourite hot foods and talk about their choices. Suggest that they make something warm to enjoy at snack time.

Look at recipe books together to find different ways of cooking potatoes. Give each child in the first group an uncooked potato and closely supervise them after you have shown the group how to pierce a potato with a fork and wrap it in foil. Explain that the foil will help to cook the potato, just like wearing a coat outdoors in winter helps to keep their bodies warm.

Put all the foil-wrapped potatoes onto a baking tray and cook them in a moderate oven for two hours or until they are soft. If necessary, use a microwave or part-bake them beforehand to save time.

Using the pre-cooked potatoes, make some cold salad with the second group of children, to contrast with the hot, oven-baked potatoes. Scoop out the potatoes from their jackets and mash them with salad cream and chopped chives. Ask the children to help you divide the mixture into small bowls.

Arrange the potato toppings on the table and ask the children which they think they would like best. Which topping is the most popular?

Remove the foil-wrapped potatoes from the oven and allow them to cool. Let each child put a chosen topping on a potato. Give each child a portion of the hot baked potato and of the cold potato salad. Ask them to compare the two types of potato dishes. Which would be the best to eat on a cold winter day?

Support
Prepare the fillings, such as grated cheese and mashed tuna, beforehand.

Extension
Make a table display of ways to keep warm on a cold day. Include items such as a hot water-bottle, gloves, scarf, hat, flask and blankets.

Small-world winter

What you need
Plastic bottles; ice-cream containers; plastic bowls of different sizes; shaving foam; small-world people; lollipop sticks; elastic bands; small plastic boxes; wooden blocks; bowl of water; towels; tiny ice-cream scoops; mustard spoons; yoghurt pots; masking tape; aprons; the photocopiable sheet on page 78.

What to do
Talk to the children about their memories of snow. Have they ever seen heavy snow? Did they try sledging or building snowmen? What do they like best about snow? Look at books and read stories about activities in the snow for those who have no experience of it.

Use a table with a washable surface and make hills and slopes with the children by taping upturned bowls and ice-cream containers to it. Cut the tops and bottoms off plastic bottles and then cut the remaining tube in half lengthways. Tape these 'slides' against the upturned containers on the table. Use the container lids to create added slopes. Spray the whole of the 'landscape' with shaving foam to create a snowy scene.

Help the children to put on aprons and encourage them to have fun with small-world people sliding, skiing and sledging up and down the slopes. Create skis from lollipop sticks and attach them to the plastic figures with elastic bands and make sledges from small boxes. Use the small spoons as spades and the yoghurt pots as buckets for digging in the 'snow'. When the children have finished playing, encourage them to wash the 'snow' off their hands and the plastic figures in a bowl of water.

Talk about the effect of the snowy winter weather on wild animals and introduce the word 'hibernation'. Talk about why and where animals hibernate. Sing the 'Winter song' and encourage the children to think of how animals will move when they are tired before their winter sleep. Role-play the actions of preparing for a long winter sleep.

Support
Encourage the children to have fun simply experiencing the pleasure of moving their hands around in the pretend snow on a washable surface without any added resources. See if they can make patterns with their fingers.

Extension
Invite the children to make a list of animals that hibernate during the winter.

Learning objective
To respond to significant experiences with a range of feelings.

Group size
Up to six children.

Home links
Make miniature sledges and skis for the children to take home and ask parents and carers to create their own small-world snow scenes with the children at home.

Jack Frost

What you need
Shiny recycled materials such as foil,
sweet-wrappers, glitter, silver crayons,
hologram paper and silver tinsel; white
and pale-blue card; PVA glue; water
tray; water; food colouring; margarine
tub; piece of sugar paper; chalk; table;
The Book of a Thousand Poems edited by
J Murray Macbain (HarperCollins).

Preparation
Freeze bowls of water and make some
ice cubes. Cut some white
and pale-blue card into
jagged 'frosty' shapes.

What to do
Take the children outside on
a frosty day or look at frosty
pictures in books and
magazines. Read the poem
'Jack Frost in the Garden'
from *The Book of a Thousand
Poems* and explain how Jack
Frost is said to be
responsible for sprinkling
frost everywhere.
   Remind the children how
cold frosty weather feels.
Help them to describe the
appearance of frost and ice,
introducing appropriate
vocabulary such as bright,
icy, shining, glittery and
silver. Put the frozen bowls
of water and ice cubes into the water
tray (leaving it for a while as ice straight
from the freezer can 'burn' skin) and
encourage the children to explore the
properties freely.
   Colour some water with food
colouring and freeze it in a margarine
tub. Tip the frozen block of ice onto a
piece of sugar paper and draw around
it with chalk. Put it back into the tub
and leave it for a while. Keep repeating
the exercise and discuss how the ice
melts and the chalk rings get smaller.

Encourage the children to talk about
changes happening to the ice. Where
do they think the ice has gone? Display
the sugar paper as a record of how the
ice melted.
   Suggest to the children that they
make 'frosty' collage pictures to display
near the water tray. Place a variety of
shiny materials in the middle of a table
and supply the white and blue 'frosty'
shapes as a base. Encourage each child
to stick their choice of materials onto

their piece of card. Mount the pictures
on black sugar paper and display them
on a background of kitchen foil.

Support
Give a smaller choice of appropriate
materials.

Extension
Ask the children to investigate how
long ice takes to melt in different
environments, for example, in water,
outside, by a heater and so on.

Winter trees

Learning objective
To concentrate for increasing lengths of time.

Group size
Six children.

What you need
Selection of magazines, books and posters with pictures of trees; samples of leaves, twigs and bark collected from outdoors; large sheet of paper; black marker pen; sugar paper; magnifying glasses; strong PVA glue.

What to do
Invite the children to look at your selection of pictures of trees and talk about the differences and similarities between the various types of trees.

Take the children to a park or woodland to observe local tree types. Do all the trees have leaves? Do some have blossom or fruit? Does the bark always look the same? Encourage the children to collect their own samples of twigs, leaves and bark to take back to your setting, reminding them that they are not allowed to pick them from the trees, only from the ground. If this is not possible, invite the children and staff to bring in appropriate samples.

Sit in a circle and ask each child in turn to show and talk about something that they have collected that comes from a tree. Is it rough or smooth? Is it hard or soft? What colour is it? Did any of the children find anything unusual such as an acorn or a pine-cone?

Place a large sheet of paper on the floor and draw the outline of a tree onto the sheet, using a black marker pen. Ask the children to look at the objects they have collected and to place them appropriately onto the tree outline, putting twigs where the branches are, bark on the trunk and so on.

Talk about the finished tree. Are all the pieces in the correct places? Have the children put leaves on the 'branches' and some on the 'ground'?

Support
Offer suggestions to the children about where their items might go on the tree outline.

Extension
Encourage the children to make individual tree collage pictures using the items collected. Let each child draw their own outline of a tree onto paper and repeat the group activity individually, sticking each item onto an appropriate place.

Home links
Ask parents and carers to take their children to a park or garden to look at different tree types and to collect items to bring to your setting.

Cinderella

What you need
Dressing-up clothes; tape recorder; cassettes tape of music to dance to; large cardboard box; pair of shiny slippers; cushion; duster; brush; garden cane; foil; card; scissors; sticky tape; paint; cleaning tools such as a broom, dustpan and cloth; the story of Cinderella.

Preparation
Invite parents and carers to donate bridesmaids' dresses for the ball-gowns and fairy's dress, and a page-boy outfit for the prince.

What to do
Obtain posters and literature about local pantomimes, including Cinderella

if possible, and use them to introduce a discussion about the pantomime season. Talk about the children's memories of pantomimes they have seen. Tell the story of 'Cinderella', emphasizing the difference between right and wrong behaviour as you introduce the actions of the characters in the story. Can the children think of someone who was kind to Cinderella? Were the ugly sisters kind or unkind?

Explain to the children that you would like them to make their own pantomime version of the story.

Make Cinderella's everyday clothes by sewing or sticking patches to a child's dress. Make a coach from a large cardboard box, cutting out windows and a door and adding a small chair. Create a wand from a garden cane and make a star out of card covered in foil. Make a cardboard clock face with the pointers at midnight.

Transform the home corner into Cinderella's house by painting a fireplace on a piece of card, attaching it to the wall and ensuring that there are cleaning tools available for Cinderella. Hang up the dressing-up clothes.

Choose another part of your setting to be the palace and have a tape recorder ready to play music. Hang the cardboard clock on the wall.

Choose children to play the various characters and help them to dress in the clothes. Read the story slowly and encourage the children to follow with appropriate actions.

When you have finished reading the story, invite the children to sit in a circle and to talk again about the actions of the characters. How did the children playing the various parts feel? Did 'Cinderella' feel different from 'the ugly sisters'? Did the sisters feel kind or unkind?

Support
Let the children play freely with the resources, making up their own stories.

Extension
Encourage the children to draw pictures and write or copy simple lines of text to create a group Cinderella story-book.

Fast food

What you need
Mixing bowl; spoon; butter; two cardamon pods; semolina; hot water; sugar; pan; small serving bowls; teaspoons.

What to do
Talk to the children about how, during the festival of Ramadan, Muslims fast during the hours of daylight. Ask the children to try and imagine how they would feel if they could not eat when they felt hungry or drink when they felt thirsty. Suggest to them that they are all going to miss out one of their snacks during a session so that they can describe what a Muslim might feel like during the festival of Ramadan.

On the chosen day, invite the children to sit in a circle at the normal snack time and remind them about why they are missing their snacks. (Do not prevent any children from drinking water if they are thirsty.) Later in the session, encourage the children to describe how they feel about missing their snacks. Do they feel hungry? Can they imagine how it would feel to miss out lunch and tea also? Explain, however, that it is not good for their bodies to fast for a long time. Give the fasting a positive outcome by using the snack money to buy food for the birds.

The next session, prepare a home-made Muslim snack, such as semolina halva. Melt 50g of butter in a pan and add the seeds of two cardamon pods. Once the butter has melted, add 125g of semolina and stir continuously until the mixture turns light brown in colour. Remove the pan from the heat and add 450ml of hot water and 125g of white sugar to the mixture. Stir the ingredients together and heat, stirring constantly until the mixture starts to boil. Let it simmer, stirring occasionally, until it starts to thicken. Pour the mixture into a large bowl and allow it to cool down. Normally, the dish would be decorated with sultanas and nuts, but these can be omitted or included as preferred. Serve the halva in the bowls and involve one of the children in distributing them. Invite the children to enjoy the halva as a snack and to remember how they felt the previous snack time, when they were 'fasting'.

Support
Give younger children a drink and simply miss out the usual fruit or biscuit accompaniment.

Extension
Suggest that the children spend the fasting time preparing some biscuits to send home as a gift to their families.

Learning objective
To respect the cultures and beliefs of others

Group size
Whole group for initial session; four children to make the semolina halva.

Home links
Send home a letter beforehand to ensure that parents and carers are aware of the reasons for the planned fast and reassured that drinks will be available.

What's in the sack?

What you need
Ready-wrapped parcels; sticky labels; felt-tipped pen; large sack; tape recorder; Christmas music; small drawstring bag; tissue; glue sticks; a copy of the photocopiable sheet on page 79 for each child.

Preparation
Wrap up a variety of objects that have easily recognizable shapes, such as a teddy bear, toy car, book and ball, and put them in a large sack. Include some

objects that make a noise when squeezed or shaken, such as a squeaky ball, a baby's rattle and a jigsaw. Number the parcels one to ten with sticky labels. Fill a small drawstring bag with tissue.

What to do
Invite the children to sit in a circle. Play the music and pass around the small drawstring 'Santa's sack' and, when the music stops, ask the child holding the bag to choose a parcel from the large sack in the centre of the circle. Encourage them to describe it to the rest of the group and guess what might be inside. Ask them to talk about the shape and size of the parcel and how it feels, and to shake it to see if it makes a noise.

Pass the parcel around so that everyone can feel it and see if they agree with what might be inside it. Put the parcel in the centre of the circle.

Continue the activity until each child has taken a parcel out of the big sack and all the parcels are in the circle. Arrange the parcels in order from 1 to 10. Starting with parcel number 1, open each one to see if the children's guesses were correct.

Give each child a copy of the photocopiable sheet and a glue stick. Ask them to cut out the parcels at the bottom of the page as close to the outline as they can and, using the glue, to stick them onto the presents in the sack to 'wrap them up'.

Support
Make the parcel shapes more obvious and play the game with just five children and parcels. Younger children can cut around the boxes on the photocopiable sheet rather than the shapes themselves.

Extension
Let the children decide who they think would like to receive each of the parcels and encourage them to write name labels beside them.

A play in a manger

What you need

A small cot or storage box; brown fabric; straw or hay; sheets of coloured material; dressing gowns; tea towels; string; walking sticks; soft animal toys; doll; three prepared crowns and gifts for 'the Three Kings'; silver star; large blanket; white sheeting; card; gold foil; shiny collage materials; book containing the story of Christmas.

What to do

Read the story of Christmas with the children to ensure that they are familiar with it. Make props to act out the story. Make some simple tabards out of sheets of coloured material. Talk about how the Three Kings brought gifts for the baby Jesus and help the children to make these presents and three crowns using card, gold foil and shiny collage materials. Transform the home area into a stable; if there are three sides, create a roof for the stable using a large blanket draped over the sides. Cover a small cot or a large shoebox with brown fabric and place straw inside. Wrap a doll in a piece of white sheeting and put it inside the home-made crib. Make a large star from card covered in silver foil and suspend it above the stable area.

Talk to the children about how baby Jesus was born in a stable. Where are babies usually born? Do they think it would be comfortable sleeping on straw in a stable?

Encourage the children to decide which part they would like to play in the dramatization and to dress themselves appropriately. Give the shepherds walking sticks for crooks and make headwear from tea towels and string. Put soft animal toys in the 'stable' around the home-made crib and invite the children to dramatize the story. Repeat the activity so that they can play different characters. Encourage them, throughout the dramatization, to manage their own dressing and undressing. Leave the props in the 'stable' so that the children can make up their own versions of the story.

Support

Encourage the children to dress freely in the clothes rather than follow a structured story.

Extension

Teach the children the words to some simple Christmas carols, such as 'Away in a Manger'.

Learning objective
To dress and undress independently.

Group size
Up to eight children.

Home links
Send home sheets of Christmas songs for parents and carers to share with their children.

Model mosques

What you need
Pictures of mosques; shoeboxes; kitchen-roll tubes cut in half; light brown or cream paint; PVA glue; coloured foil; plastic mousse pots; carpet scraps; small-world figures; fabric scraps.

What to do
Visit or look at pictures of a mosque and make comparisons with other places of worship with which the children are familiar. Talk about the festival of Eid-ul-Fitr and the significance of the mosque to Muslims during this festival. Suggest that the children create models of mosques.

Ask each child to choose a shoebox for the main building shape and to paint it light brown or cream. Use coloured foil for windows and cut an opening for the door. Cut out a piece of carpet for the floor. Cut small slits in one end of a kitchen-roll tube and fold the card out so that it can be glued easily to the lid of the box to create the minaret from which Muslims are called to prayer. Show each child how to secure an upturned mousse pot to the lid to form the dome of the mosque, symbolizing the heavens. Paint the tube and dome with paint mixed with PVA glue and attach star-shaped and moon-shaped pieces of foil to the top of the dome.

Show the children pictures of other places of worship such as a church or synagogue. How do these buildings compare to the children's model mosques? Are all the buildings the same shape? Do they have a spire or tower and coloured windows? Look at pictures and talk to the children about what happens inside the mosque. Discuss the differences in seating between the Christian churches with rows of pews, and mosques with just a carpet for people to kneel and pray on. Use scraps of fabric to dress small-world people in robes in the style of Muslims attending the mosque.

Support
Provide the children with ready-made model mosques.

Extension
Invite the children to make Eid cards with you. Decorate them with simple mendhi patterns, moons and stars. Remember that these cards open from left to right.

EARLY YEARS AROUND THE YEAR Personal, social and emotional development

Resolutions

Learning objective
To consider the consequences of their words and actions for themselves and others.

Group size
Ideal for a 'circle time' discussion followed by smaller groups of six for the main activity.

What you need
Paper; paint; paintbrushes; felt-tipped pens.

What to do
Talk to the children about the significance of the new year as a time when people reflect on the past year and look forward to a fresh start by making new plans. What events can the children recall from last year? Look at photograph albums as reminders of the special times as well as the everyday activities that took place. Discuss New Year celebrations that take part in other cultures and explain that some people like to clean out their houses in preparation for the coming year.

Discuss New Year resolutions with the children and talk about some of the changes that people make in their lives, for example, becoming more healthy by taking regular walks and eating fewer sweets. Ask the children to suggest resolutions that they could make to improve their own lives, such as keeping their bedrooms tidy, helping to look after a younger brother or sister, or sharing toys.

Encourage each child in turn to talk to the rest of the group about their chosen resolution. Together, discuss the resolutions and how they will affect others either at home or at your setting.

Ask each child to draw or paint a picture to depict their chosen resolution, and act as scribe to write an appropriate caption for each picture. Attach all the finished pictures together to form a large display book of resolutions. Read the book regularly with the children to see whether they have remembered to continue their proposed actions.

Support
Help the children to think of small manageable changes that they can make, such as remembering to wash their hands before meals.

Extension
Talk to the children about the Hogmanay traditions associated with New Year in Scotland. For example, explain that 'first footing' is when significant items are brought into the house by the first person to enter in the new year. Dance to some traditional Scottish dance music, eat oakcakes for a snack and join hands as staff sing 'Auld Lang Syne'.

Learning objective
To work as part of a
group, taking turns
and sharing fairly.

Group size
Up to six children
depending on the
game played.

Find the honey

What you need
A selection of children's
board games; two dice,
one with colours and
one with numbers; the
photocopiable sheet on
page 80; card;
laminator.

Preparation
Make several copies of
the photocopiable sheet
on card and laminate
them.

What to do
Talk about the Japanese
festival of Ganjitsu and
the traditions associated
with it, such as
receiving money from
relatives, eating special foods, wearing
special clothes and playing games with
the family. Are the festival traditions
similar to those of festivals that the
children have experienced, such as
birthdays? Talk about the children's
favourite indoor and outdoor games.

Arrange a display of board games on
a table, look at them together and then
play some of the games. Choose a child
to go to the table and select the first
game. Play it together, emphasizing the
need to take turns and wait for others.
Talk about how it feels to win and lose,
stressing that the fun is in playing
together. Discuss the importance of
being happy for the winner and not
feeling sad about losing.

Suggest to the children that they
might like to make their own game.
Show them the gameboard made from
the photocopiable sheet and ask them
to find things to make counters, such as
small plastic bears. Explain that the
counters will need to match the colours
on the dice. Encourage the children to
play the game in groups of three.

Explain that they should throw both the
dice and move the counter that
corresponds to the colour on the first
dice along the number of spaces that is
shown on the second dice. Ask the
children to try and invent rules for a
new game to play using the
photocopiable sheet. For example, they
could use a numbered dice and miss a
turn if they land on a number where
two paths cross.

Support
Play a non-competitive game with
younger children using the
photocopiable sheet and putting
coloured dot stickers on the faces of a
dice to match the colours of small
plastic bears. Ask them to throw the
dice and move the correct coloured
bear along one square. A bear will be
the winner rather than a child.

Extension
Invite the children to make up their
own gameboard using a large sheet of
paper and felt-tipped pens.

Home links
Ask parents and
carers to bring in
simple board games
to play with the
children or to come
and help with their
home-made games.

Take heart

What you need

Cornflour; salt; spoon; pan; water; red food colouring; rolling-pins; heart-shaped pastry cutters (one large and one small); pencil or straw; string or ribbon; glitter; sequins; PVA glue; oven tray; greaseproof paper; safety-pins; strong tape.

What to do

Talk about St Valentine's Day, a time when people give cards and gifts to loved ones. Suggest that the children might like to make heart-shaped gifts for someone who is special to them. To make the pendants, put 125g of cornflour and 250g of salt into a pan and let the children take turns to mix together the dry ingredients. Add 350ml of cold water and a few drops of red food colouring. Stir the mixture together and cook on a medium heat, away from the children, stirring until the mixture forms a smooth, thick dough. Tip the dough onto a flat surface and leave it to cool. Give each child a small amount of the cooled dough mixture and a rolling-pin. Ask them to roll out the dough until it is flat and to cut out a large heart shape to create the first stage of the pendant. Once they have done this, hand around the smaller heart-shaped cutters with which to remove the centre of the large heart. Ask each child to keep the smaller heart shape cut from the centre to make a badge. Help them to pierce a hole in the top of the pendant with a pencil or straw. Place the pendant and smaller heart shapes onto a sheet of greaseproof paper on a large baking tray. Bake them in a cool oven for 1 to 2 hours and then leave them to cool in a safe place.

Give the children their pendants and small hearts and ask them to paint them with PVA glue and sprinkle on glitter and sequins. Help each child to thread a ribbon or string through their pendant, and tape a safety-pin to the back of their small heart to make a badge.

Support

Ask the children to only make the heart-shaped badges.

Extension

Invite the children to make decorative presentation boxes for the gifts using recycled cardboard and foil.

Learning objective
To form good relationships with peers.

Group size
Six children.

Home links
Let the children make pendants and badges to take home for special family members.

Sweet treats

What you need
Mixing bowl; spoon; plate; oil; frying pan; plain and self-raising flour; four eggs; milk; water; pancake fillings such as chocolate spread, syrup, sugar and lemon juice.

What to do
Talk to the children about Shrove Tuesday, the day before the start of Lent when Christians remember the 40 days and nights that Jesus travelled through the wilderness. Discuss how Christians like to clear out their cupboards and prepare for Lent, a time when they give up certain things. To use up some of these items, pancakes are usually cooked on this day.

Involve the children in all stages of the preparation of the pancake mixture. Put two cups of plain flour into a mixing bowl. Gradually add milk until the mixture forms a thick paste. Beat quickly until the mixture is smooth and without lumps. Add the two eggs to the thick mixture and allow each child to take a turn at stirring. If needed, add some cold water to thin the mixture. Heat a frying pan and pour in a little cooking oil. Talk about the dangers of hot pans and oil with the children and ensure that they watch from a distance. Pour enough mixture to coat the base of the pan and allow it to cook. When the under-side starts to go brown, flip the pancake over and let the other side

cook. Slide the pancake onto a plate. Repeat until all the mixture is used. Give each child a pancake and encourage them to spread their chosen topping onto it before rolling it up and eating it.

Repeat the pancake mixing process using self-raising flour to make a thicker mixture. Pour smaller quantities of the mixture into the pan, creating smaller, thicker circles roughly 8cm in diameter. Ask the children to compare the two types of pancake. Did the pancakes taste the same? Which mixture made the thickest pancakes?

Support
Help the children to spread their chosen fillings onto their pancakes.

Extension
Invite the children to do a survey to find out which pancake and filling each child in the group preferred. Make a wall chart to show preferred fillings and pancake types.

Caring for seeds

Find the baby

Fun with eggs

Five Easter eggs

Five Easter eggs in the cupboard by the door,
A little mouse nibbled one so that left four.

Four Easter eggs, I do hope there's one for me,
My sister came and took one and ate it after tea.

Three Easter eggs, wrapped in silver, red and blue,
One rolled down from the shelf and that left two.

Two Easter eggs, soon they will all be gone,
My brother came and took one and that left only one.

Now there's one lovely egg waiting on the shelf,
I know what I'll do, I'll eat it all myself!

Jean Evans

Easter is here!

(Tune: 'Frère Jacques')

Easter bunnies, Easter bunnies,
Hop around, hop around,
Looking for their burrows, looking for their burrows,
In the ground, in the ground.

New born lambs skip, new born lambs skip,
See them run, see them run,
Chasing one another, chasing one another,
Having fun, having fun.

Hard-boiled eggs, hard-boiled eggs,
Roll around, roll around,
Racing down the hill now, racing down the hill now,
Without a sound, without a sound.

Easter chickens, Easter chickens,
Watch them hatch, watch them hatch,
Fluffing out their feathers, fluffing out their feathers,
Scritch and scratch, scritch and scratch.

Jean Evans

Maypole dancing

EARLY YEARS AROUND THE YEAR Personal, social and emotional development

Pack a suitcase

A fruity surprise

Caring for pets

Dragon drama

(Tune: 'Here We Go Round the Mulberry Bush')

1. Here we come row-ing dra-gon boats, dra-gon boats, dra-gon boats.

Here we come row-ing dra-gon boats at Dra-gon Boat Fes-ti-val time.

2. This is how we pull the oars,
Pull the oars, pull the oars.
This is how we pull the oars
At Dragon Boat Festival time.

3. This is how we ride the waves,
Ride the waves, ride the waves.
This is how we ride the waves
At Dragon Boat Festival time.

Sally Scott

EARLY YEARS AROUND THE YEAR Personal, social and emotional development

Doctor Foster

Dr Foster went to Gloucester
In a shower of rain;
He stepped in a puddle,
Right up to his middle,
And never went there again!

Traditional

Fun with apples

All aglow

Harvest basket

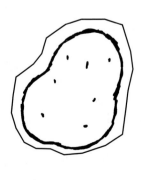

EARLY YEARS AROUND THE YEAR Personal, social and emotional development

Day and night

Winter song

(Tune: 'If You're Happy and You Know It')

1. I'm a big brown bear and I'm tired, I'm a

big brown bear and I'm tired. I need to hi-ber-nate, I

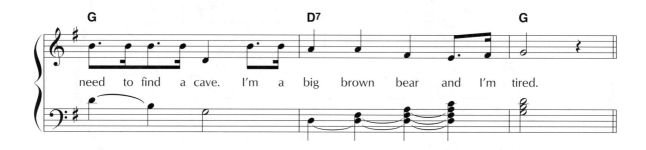

need to find a cave. I'm a big brown bear and I'm tired.

2. I'm a shiny black cat and I'm tired,
I'm a shiny black cat and I'm tired.
I need to hibernate and I'm hanging
    upside-down.
I'm a shiny black cat and I'm tired.

3. I'm a curly shelled snail and I'm tired,
I'm a curly shelled snail and I'm tired.
I'm a curly shelled snail, looking for a
    sheltered wall.
I'm a curly shelled snail and I'm tired.

4. I'm a prickly hedgehog and I'm tired,
I'm a prickly hedgehog and I'm tired.
I'm a prickly hedgehog, looking for a pile
    of leaves.
I'm a prickly hedgehog and I'm tired.

5. I'm a spotted ladybird and I'm tired,
I'm a spotted ladybird and I'm tired.
I'm a spotted ladybird, finding shelter with
    my friends.
I'm a spotted ladybird and I'm tired.

Sally Scott

What's in the sack?

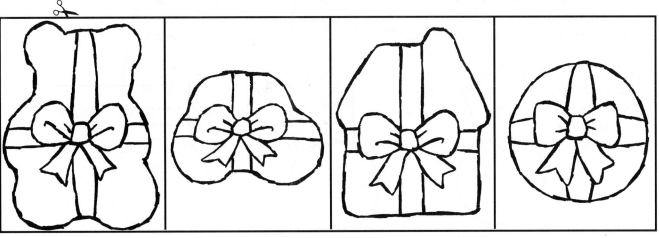

Find the honey